TRIBAL PEOPLE AND INDIAN CIVILIZATION

DR. SUDIP BHUI | DR. SAVITA MISHRA | DR. SANJAY KUMAR CHOUDHARY

Contents

Preface

'Unity is strength' is very popular and established proverb for building a nation. Present and coming days are with numerous problems of disintegration, violence and conflict. India is vast country, inhabitant of a notable part of world population along with great variety of morphological, cultural and geo-historical nature. Integration and peace is also more challenging to get a united nation. To know each other we have to delve, understand and feeling "self" for all the communities of our country. In this series of research outcomes we make an endeavor to glorify our tribal brethren throughout their history and present time.

Categorization of people is serious matter in respect to origin, distinct cultures, society and cultures, but in history of human civilization is completely impossible to understand without discussion this challenge. Each and every group of people has their own genius, skills, traditions and heritage. In spite of controversies in definitions, concepts and dialogues the contributions tribal people is very much essential to build a good nation.

In the pre-colonial period, we can call all the people who have traditionally lived in certain lands, with distinct languages, cultures, social customs and nature friendly as tribal people. More than 370 million people carry this tradition in more than 70 countries all over the world. Compared to the world history, the traditional trend of indigenous people in our country is obvious.

As a follower of the geniuses of the Indus Valley Civilization, in the *Rik veda*, in the Ramayana and in the Mahabharata in 1600 BC, in the Arthashastra of Kautilya in 320 BC, according to the thirteenth inscription of Mahamati Ashoka, they were active in an ancient history in India and South Asia. In the middle Ages, the good governance of the Munda, Asura, Nag and Bheel many tribal dynasties in central and northern India signified a glorious trends. During the Mughal and British rule, they fought for the protection of their habitat, nature and dignity. The Malpahariya, Chuar and Pike Rebellions, Kol Rebellion, Santal Rebellion and Munda Rebellion have played a leading role in the continuous movement of India's independence struggle. The world map shows the history of the great struggles of Indigenous peoples in the United States, Canada, and Mexico, Brazil, etc. in the Amazon region.

The contribution of indigenous peoples to science, technology, art and literature in world civilization has been everlasting. The world famous female mathematician of America's Chiroki indigenous peoples, and the engineer Marigold Ross of rocket Science, the US military, played a key role in NASA's work plan. John Herrington of the Chickas indigenous peoples of America participated in NASA – Sixteenth Shuttle Mission, 2002 and went to space. Susan Picotti from the Omaha indigenous group in America became the first doctor to open the first hospital in the area. Joana Senadoya a famous singer, composer and guitarist from the American Onneida group, has received the Grammy Award with numerous accolades, besides; famous singer Pura Fey has received Community Spirit Award. Even Hollywood's one-time highest – earning actress and one time academic and three time golden globe award winning actress Angelina Jolie is of indigenous descent.

In our India and the people of the indigenous community continue to make important contributions to the national services, Mr. Girish Chandra Murmu coming from a remote village of Orissa takes over charge as Comptroller and Auditor General of India, Mrs. Draupadi Murmu has completed his term as governor of Jharkhand and become first representative of tribal people as President of India, Karia Munda of Jharkhand got Padmabhushan, Digambar Hansda of Tatanagar and Kamala Pujari of Koraput have received Padmashri awards for their special contribution in the field of agriculture, literatures and academics.

A lot of instances about large contribution of indigenous people are found in world history. Still a notable section of world people think tribal people live in an isolated and backward region and want to remain aloof from main stream of civilization. This proposed volume will make effort to create interest for research, studies and enquiries about the role models of tribal people.

A group of young researchers under supervision of the editors tried with their ceaseless efforts through fieldwork, library work and interactions among themselves. Tribal religion is animism in feature, is harmonized with nature and more sustainable than other advance phase of religion. As integrated phase of their social cultural life, religion always expresses its pristine tendency. Its impact comes in worshipping to sacred groves, helpful to conservation of rare quality of plant species throughout entire phase of their life. Literature is reflections of socio-cultural life of these aboriginals. Their writings are analyzed in perspective of their thoughts feelings and sentiments. Agriculture is still major means of economic operation of our country, tribal people by their traditional practices has had golden treasure of experiences and knowledge for sustainable agriculture. Moreover, agricultural cycle is involved with their entire gamut of social cultural life, especially in festivals. Education of tribal people is not escaped from the harsher effect of COVID 19, in this scope the educational problem is discussed in a tribal belt. Sports have quickest effect of excellence with physical capacities as well as practices and hard work, give acknowledgement and status to one nation among the international platforms. Here contributions and prospects of tribal people in this domain are discussed with specific personal case studies. For examining the future India, tribal people are coming with leading role in our great nation, which reflects in our one of the articles. In this way this volume offers to its reader a multi dimensional tradition, transformation and emerging capacities of tribal people to build and excelled one stronger India.

This little effort is not a complete versions in any of the attempts but it is sure that new ideas and thought provoking role will ushered among the mind of future researchers. Past, present and future are not isolated facts but scenarios of continuous efforts and deeds. Our efforts will be come in little success in future when many scholars will be busy in searching more and more contributions of marginal, downtrodden parts of our population in origin, building and development of our nation.

Dr. Sudip Bhui
Dr. Savita Mishra
Dr. Sanjay Kumar Choudhary

Ethno-Medicinal Practices among Santal Tribe of Purulia District, West Bengal, India

Latu Lal Mahata: Research Scholar, Department of Anthropology and Tribal Studies, Sidho-Kanho-Birsha University, Purulia, West Bengal, India.

Dr. Sudip Bhui: Assistant Professor, Department of Anthropology and Tribal Studies, Sidho-Kanho-Birsha University, Purulia, West Bengal, India.

Abstract: Plants have being been used as a medicine since ancient period in all over the world and India is one of the treasure house of the ethno medicine. Indigenous peoples are still using the plants from the beginning of their life. According to the census 2011, Santals are the numerically dominated in West Bengal among the other tribal population (total population 2,280,540; 1.8%). The present study was conducted to collect information about their disease type, ethno-medicinal plants and other materials used to by Santals tribe at Brajarajpur village under Barabazar block of Purulia District, West Bengal. Anthropological tools like interview, observation, photography, schedule methods etc. were used to collect the primary data to investigate their ethno medicinal practices from the three ethno-medicine men as well as Ojhas. Now days they are depend on ethno-medicines and rituals as primary health care necessities and these medicines mostly used to cure the urinal disease, poison bites, liver disease, skin disease etc. Their folk medicine knowledge is not only to save money and side effects of modern drugs but also the ethno-medicines are used to improve their healthcare system. 34 plants were recorded which they used as a medicine. The present study tried to explore the uses of ethno-medicines and conservationof important medicinal plants of the study area.

Key words: *Ethno-medicine, medicinal plants, disease, ethno-medicinal men, Santal, healthcare*

Introduction: Disease or infirmity is a common character of human health though it is happened due to any reason. In ancient world human was dependent only on the forest that indicates ethno medicine for their taking treatment were used to cure from disease and that trend still flowing today but that type of treatment have become less. After day by day it has modified and changed into allopathic, homeopathic and ayurbedic medicine but yet many people are taking ethno-medicine. We are known to all that health is wealth. Health is "A status of complete physical, mental and social well-being and not merely the absence of disease or infirmity" (WHO, 1948). Health in relationship with a variety of factors such as the individual's physical, social, psychological, and emotional condition; environmental and cultural factors, as well as the creativity and productivity of a person. Ethno-medicine plays an important role in a health care practices among ethnic group. Indigenous peoples are still using the plants from the beginning of their life.). According to the census 2011, the Santals are the numerically dominated in West Bengal among the total Scheduled Tribes population (total population 2,280,540; 51.8%). Paucity of hospital facilities and expert allopathic doctors in tropical area, any destruction of tropical forests is destroying the primary healthcare network involving local plants and traditional health curer (Ballik, 1996). According to the Red list of threatened species, 204 plant species are being endanger state in India (McNeely et al, 2001).

Plants have traditionally been used for treatment of human in different ethnic and social groups. However, this valuable source of knowledge is not adequately documented, which impedes their widespread use, evaluation and validation. The wide spread use of use of traditional medicine could be attributed to cultural acceptability, economic affordability and efficacy certain type of diseases as compared to modern medicine. Thus different local communities in country across the world have indigenous knowledge in various medicinal plants where they use their perception and experience to use their plants and parts of pants to be used when dealing with different ailments. The dependence of the plant based health care system could partly be attributed to underdeveloped infrastructure and modern medical health care system in general area.

Ethno-medicine/ Folk medicine

Folk medicine, methods of curing by means of healing objects, herbs, or animal parts; ceremony; conjuring, magic or witchcraft, and other means apart from the formalised practice of medical science. In nearly all ancient and preliterate societies disease and death were and are attributed to the workings of malevolent beings, spirits, or forces. Complex ritual and medicinal applications were devised to heal these ills. This testifies the fact that folk medicine is not exclusive to people of lower socio-economic class and illiterate peoples as commonly believed. The concepts and practices in folk medicines are based upon the humeral theories, cosmological speculations, magic in learned/oral medicine and religion. The practice field of this medicine is midwifery, bone setting, supernatural cures of various types with main emphasis is on utilizing natural herbs, roots, plants and other natural things in a given eco-system. The knowledge of such medicinal plants and preparation of medicine are still handed down mostly in oral form to the next generation of such practitioners [Chaudhuri, 1986; Reddy, 19861.]

There has been an increase of demand in international trade because herbal medicines which are the result of research of ethno -medicine are very effective, cheaply available, supposedly have no side effects and used as alternative to allopathic medicines.

Materials and methods:

The present study was conducted Brajarajpur village under Barabazar Block of Purulia district, West Bengal during February to march, 2016. This village is situated 300 km. away from Kolkata, capital city of West Bengal. For this study, data were collected from three ethno-medicinal men as well as ojhas to know the name of the ethno-medicinal plants, procedure to prepare medicine and cure days from diseases by which diseases Santals were attacked. A face to face interview methodology was used for these data collection. Observation tool were applied to see prepare medicine and to identify some medicinal plants. Unstructured scheduled were also applied to record the name of the disease, name of the medicinal plants etc.

Map of the study area

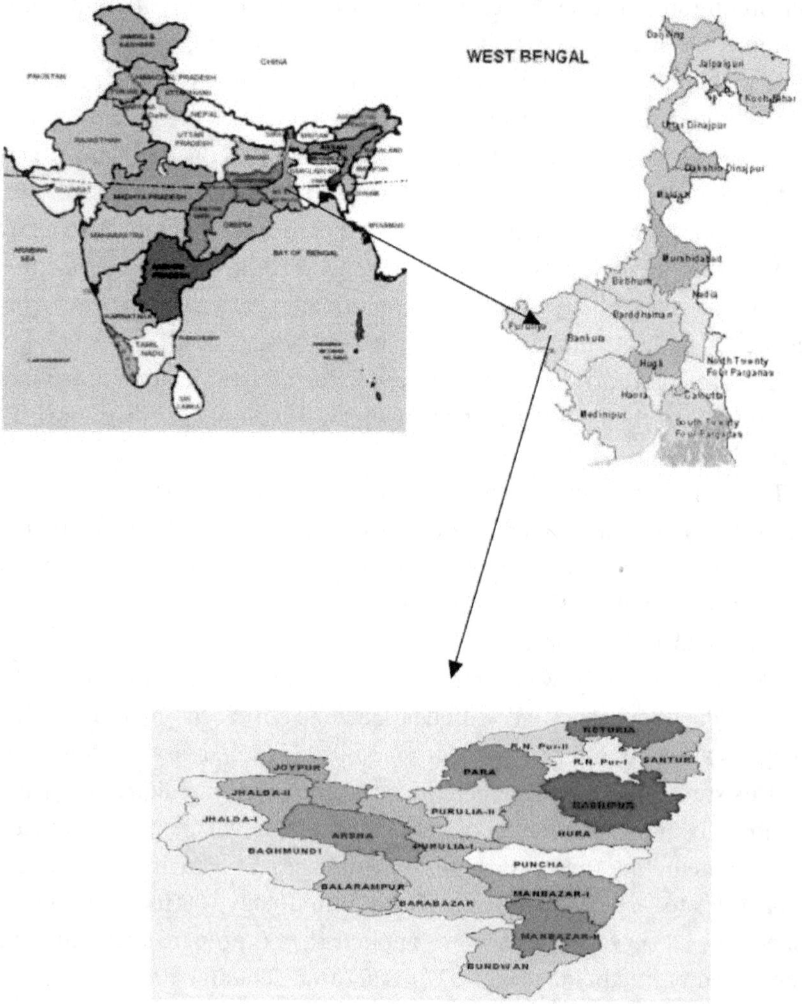

Barabazar block

Objectives:

The main objectives of the study is to search the relationship between Folk medicine or Ethno medicine practices and their health care and to document medicinal plants used by Santal tribe as a medicine and the procedures of preparing ethno-medicine for treatment of diseases.

Findings and discussion:

The table:1 reveals the 25 disease's local name, english name and their symtoms which were collected from three Ojhas. Ethno-medicine was applied for treatment of mentioned diseases (table:1) to the patient. Scientific name of the medicinal plants were also included by searching in google and others sources.

Table : 1 name of diseases, symptoms, raw material used and cured time according the their perpective

SL. No	Local name of diseases.	English name of diseases or illness.	Symptoms of the patient.	Name of raw material and procedure to prepare medicine.	Scientific name of medicinal plants and animals	Periods of cure
1	Karamet	Blindness	Patient can't see clearly, but the sight is vague	The *karam leaves are to be crashed, and then it is added to clarified butter. Then the mixed solution is to be used on the eyes with bandage.	*Nauclea parvifolia.	5-10 days
2	Andhua or Ratkana	Night Blindness	Patient can't see at night but clearly see at day.	*The leaves of Andrographis are grinded and prepared medicine.	*Andrographis peniculata.	25-30 days
3	Toa jorhote lutur bele	Ear Suppuration	The patient is short of hearing due to filled earwax causes of pain in the ear.	Dwarfish The *metal leaves are to be made hotter and then this solution is to be used on the affected area.	*Terminalia catappa	15-20 days
4	Lutur Kala	Deafness	The patient do not derive hear	Dwarfish the *datura fruit are to be mixed with **mustard oil. Then it is kept fire to make hot. Then this solution is used.	*Datura stramonium. **Brassica nigra.	10-15 days
5	Lutur Hasu	Ear ache	The patient feels very painful in the ear due to	The juice of *Ashoka leaves are use	* Saraca asoka.	5-7 days

			severe cold.			
6	Datrisi	Bleeding of the gums	Some slash are come out in the gap of two teeth, when it is come out, it is very painful and that time come out blood.	Wash the teeth by salt, also use hot water.		Till the end of gums.
7	Jaundice	Jaundice	Urine are yellow, nail, body and eyes are slidely yellow.	Take the juice of *pigeon pea leaves and mixed the **mastered oil and then rubs in the body.	*Cajanus cajan **Brassica nigra.	7 days
8	Kom Kom	Mumps	To catch cold the glands are to be swellide ear and that place are very painful	The 'Bakhar' are pulverized and then mixed with the #honey and then used the painful places.	#Apis mellifera	5-7 days
9	Dad	Ring warm	A roundish strain is seen on the skin.	*Basil leaves and salt are mixed and then it used in affected area.	*Ocimum basilicum.	10-15 days
10	Talsa	Measles	Mouth sore	#Femy milk one drop and *kadamba bark	#Ovis aries *Nedamarckia cadamba.	11-13 days

11	Sada srab	White colored urine	Comes out hormone by urine	Branches of *pinewheelflower tree, **tarmaric, ***cumin seeds and ****black peper in the morning	*Tabernaemontana divaricata. **curcuma longa. ***Cuminum cymium. ****piper nigrum.	7 days
12	Bing gar	Snake bite	Snake bite people are slowly sensless and came out the 'fan' (local term) with mouth.	This people are brought out the Manasa Devi and invoked and then ojha gives him jharuni.		1days
13	kharak Muth	Graval	Blood come out by urine	*Red lily flower-1 pice, **mango bark-25gm, ***cumin seed 10gm, ****black peper 10gm, and smashed are mixed and make tablet	*Nymphaca nouchali. **Mangifera indica' ***Cuminum cymium. ****piper nigrum.	7 days
14	Kar ghao	Chronic scabies	Smell sore on the body	Mixed the ranjan and *Tiger claw fruit oil.	*Martynia annua.	15-20 days
15	kurham Hasu	Pain in the chest	Pain in the whole chest	#Cow oil, ##gohi oil and ###Hingaraj oil mixed and massage on the whole body.		5-7 days
16	Mu Khaj mayang	Bleeding by nose	Some time blood come out with nose	Take smell of dung		3-5 days

	jarang Kana					
17		Muscular pain from ouer exertion	So pain in the whole body musles for hard work	The patient uses *Hophead flower leaves.	*Barlerialupulina	10-15 days
18	.Danda hasu	Pain in the loins	Pain in the loins when are sited down and others	*RonJono's roots and salt are mixed with **mustard oil and after doing low heat, the mixture are used in the pain area.	**Brassica nigra.	7 days
19	Khug	Cough	To catch cold in the body the cough come out with mouth.	*European black night shade fruit and clarified butter	*Solanum americanum.	7 days
20	Eksira	Hydrosele		Clarified butter and salt are mixed and uses the painfull places.		5 days
21	Adh kapali	Forehead pain	Pain in the one side of forehead	*Gulattar bark-one piece and **Clove two piece are mixed with the bark of *the peepal tree and prepared medicine.	*Tinospora sinensis **Syzygium aromaticum ***Ficus religiosia.	3 days

22	Inbor re bemari	Dyspepsia	The patient feel dizziness, vomiting and headache	Three leaves of *Centella, salt-5 g.m, sugar-5 gm are mixed and then are prepared medicine.	*Centella asiatica	3-4 days
23	Mada	Runny nose	Water come out anytime from nose.	10 gm* black gram and 3 piece **garlic are grind together and embrocate in the whole body.	*Vinga mungo **Allium sativum	5-7 days
24	Bale gidra goh	Diarrhea		*Coco grass, **vabri dal and ***Citrus are mixed and then are eaten every day.	*Cyperus rotundus ***Citrus aurantifolia	3-5 days
25	Ula	acidity	vomiting	Three Leaves of *neem, **bel leaves-1piece, ***turmeric-10 gm, and ****sugar 10 gm are grind together and the solution are drunk with water in the morning.	*Azadiracata indica, **Aegle mormelos, ***curcuma longa ****sucrose	3days

*=name of medicinal plants and their scientific name, #= name of animals and their scientific name

A total of 34 plants and other some materials were recorded as raw materials and scientific name of the medicinal plants (Table-1: column no. 5 & 6 respectively). The table:1 demonstrates that 25 types of diseases or illness were found. Ethno-medicine was applied to cure from diseases or illness as a primary health care. Most of the diseases or illnesses were ear, eye, skin and pain related. Besides these santals tribe took treatment for jaundice, cough, acidity, urinal problem and liver related problem. According to the ethno-medicine men, ethno-medicine was very effective for urinal problem and this problem could not complcte by allopathic doctor. For any type of diseases of the Santals, firstly they take ethno medicine from the medicine man and if the patient is not cured then they decide to take other type of treatment. Maximum medicines are prepared with leaves and fruits of the plants. Mainly these medicine are mostly used to cure urinary problem, skin disease, verities pain disease, jaundice, cough, acidity, measles, blindness etc.

The medicines were prepared with the leaves, roots, fruit, bark, flower, fruit-oil of the plants. Leaves-28.57%, fruit-25.71%, fruit-oil 17.14%, bark-8.57%, flower 8.57%, roots-5.71% and stem-5.71% of the finding medicinal plants are used as a medicine (Figure:1). Leaves of plants were used maximum to prepare medicine. Another study on Santals tribe of Bankura district in West Bengal conducted by Chowdhury and Karmakar, 2016 found the same result that leaves were maximum used for preparing medicine. Stems as well as roots of plants were less used to prepare medicine. These parts of medicinal plants collect from near forest and grassy land. Some implements are collect near glossary or market.

Figure 1: parts of medicinal plants used by Santal tribe.

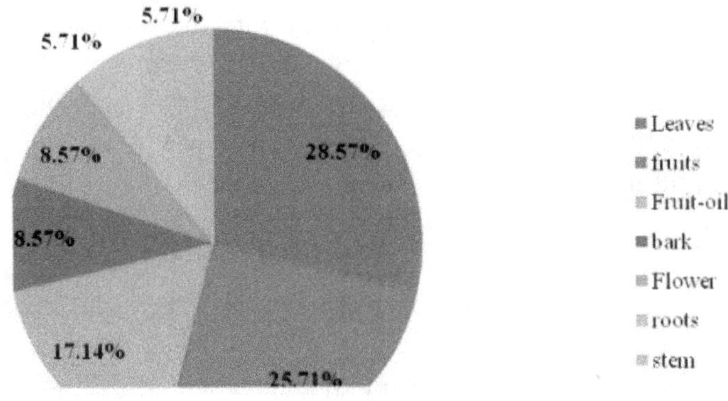

Verities type of medicine applies i.e. massaging oil, dry pill or raw pill as disease or illness type. Pleasurably medicinal person gives dust of the plants to the patient as a medicine. The patient eats this medicine maximum for one month. Medicinal persons use other things which are produces from livestock. When the patient eats Medicine the medicinal persons strictly forbid to eat some foods. Suppose if any patient have attracted with Urinal problem then ojha forbid to eat to meat, fish, eag, onion, ginger and garlic. The ojha said "if you dn't obey the food taboo than you will not cure from disease". The ojhas said that the patients were decreasing to take this medicine now days. Maximum patient were going to show specialist allopathic doctor.

Conclusion:

Their folk medicinal knowledge is not only to save money and side effects from modern drugs but also the ethno-medicines are used to improve their healthcare system. The traditional knowledge of herbal medicine practiced among the Santal community of the Brajarajpur village of Barabazar block of Purulia district should be conserved through its documentation before it is lost from the respective Santal societies forever. The study can be used to develop new cost effective herbal drug. This study will helpful to conduct research on these trees by medicinal researcher. It will help preparing a detail inventory of ethno medicine. The use of quantitative tools is very new approach here in analysis of Santal health care practices among the Santals of Purulia district of West Bengal. It will help preparing a detail inventory of ethno medicine. . Unless the plants are conserved and ethno medicinal knowledge is documented there is a loss that both the valuable medicinal plants and the associated indigenous knowledge of ethnic group are vanished forever due to lack of documentation and loss of medicinal plants due to population pressure agricultural ex-pension and deforestation as well as drought, urbanisation and acculturation.

Reference:

Acharya J and Mukherjee A. (2010). Herbal therapy for urinary ailments as documented from Bankura district (West Bengal). Indian J Sci Res, 1(1):67-69.

Archer W.G. (1984). "Tribal Law and Justice",ICSSR

Balick M.J. (1996).Transforming ethnobotany for the new millenium. Ann Missouri botanical garden. Ann Missouri Bot Garden; 83: 58-66.

Bandopadhyay PK. (1998). "Tribal Situation in Eastern India", Subarnarekha, Kolkata.

Banerjee A., Mukherjee A., Sinhababu A. (2013). Ethnobotanical documentation of some wild edible plants in Bankura District, West Bengal, India. J Ethno Trad Med Photon, 585-590.

Basak S.K. (1997). Medicinal plants of Bankura (W.B.) and their uses, *J Natl Bot Soc*, 61.

Basu R. (2003). Ethnomedicinal information of yellow flowered palash and silk coton in Bankura district of West Bengal. J Econ Taxon Bot, 27(3): 580-581.

Bodding P.O. (1925). "Studies in Santal Medice and Connected Folklore", Asiatic Society, Kolkata – 16.

Bodding P.O. (reprint 2013). "Tradition and Institution of the Santal", Gyan Publishing House, New Delhi.

Bompass C.H. (1981). "Folklore of Santal Parganas", Ajoy Book Service, New Delhi.

Byg A. and Balsev H. (2001). Diversity and use of palms in Zahamena, eastern Madagascar. Biodivers Conserv, 10: 951- 970.

Chaudhuri R.H.N., Saren A.M., Molla H.A. (1982). Some less known uses of plants from the tribal areas of Bankura district, West Bengal, *Indian Mus Bull*, 14- 71.

Choudhary S.N. (2012). "Tribal Health and Nutrion", Rawat Publication, Jaipur 202004.

Choudhuri R.H.N., Soren AM., Mollah A. (1982). Some less known uses of plants from the tribal areas of Bankura district, West Bengal. Indian Mus Bull,14: 71-73.

Chowdhury H.R. and Karmakar S. 2015. Ethnomedicine of Santal tribe living around Susunia hill of Bankura district, West Bengal, India: The quantitative approach. Journal of Applied Pharmaceutical Science Vol. 5 (02), pp. 127-136. DOI: 10.7324/JAPS.2015.50219

Deepak A. and Anshu S. (2008) Indigenous Herbal Medicines: TribalFormulations and Traditional Herbal Practices. Aavishkar Publishers Distributor, Jaipur.

Ghosh A. (1999). Herbal veterinary from the tribal areas of Bankura District, West Bengal. J. Econ. Taxon. Bot, 23(2): 557-560.

Ghosh A., Maity S., Maity M. (1996). Ethnomedicine in Bankura district, West Bengal, *J Econ Taxon Bot, Addl Ser*, 12- 318.

Ghosh R.B. & Das D. (1999). A preliminary census and systematic survey of antidiabetic plants of Midnapore district, West Bengal, India, *J Econ Taxon Bot*, 23, 535.

Kalla A.K. & Joshi PC. (2004). "Tribal Health and Medicine", Concept Publishing House, New Delhi – 59

Maiti A, MannaCK. (2001). Indigenous medicines used by the Santal people of the Panchet hill region of the District Puruliya, West Bengal, for the control of fertility. Curare, 24:137-141.

Maiti A. and Manna C.K. (2000). Ethno medicines used by the Santal of Baghmundi-Ajodhya Hillregion of the Puruliya District, West Bengal, in controlling the fertility. Ethnobotany, 12: 72-76.

McNeely G.A., Miller KR., Reid WV., Mittermeier R.A., Werner T.R. Conserving the world's biological diversity. Michigan: IUCN; 2001.

Namhata D. & Ghosh A. (1993).Herbal folk medicines of Bankura district, West Bengal, *Geobios, New Rep*, 12- 94.

Namhata D. & Mukherjee A. (1988). Ethnomedicine in Bankura district, West Bengal, *Indian J Appl Pure Biol*, 3- 53.

Troisi J. (1979). "Tribal Religion; Religious Beliefs and practices among the Santals", Manohar Publishers & Distributors, New Delhi – 110002

CHAPTER TWO

Contribution of Tribal Genius in Leading Development Sectors of India

Nayan Ruhidas: Research Scholar of Anthropology & Tribal Studies, Sidho Kanho Birsha University, Purulia

Piu Mahali: Research Scholar of Anthropology & Tribal Studies, Sidho Kanho Birsha University, Purulia

Dr. Sudip Bhui: Assistant Professor, Department of Anthropology & Tribal Studies, Sidho Kanho Birsha University, Purulia

Abstract

The Research paper is an attempt to highlight the contribution of tribal talent in India's leading development sectors and to encourage tribal people to contribute to the development of the country. The total size of the sample is 40 indigenous people of India who made important contributions to the national service. The people were chosen by random sampling method. Some case studies of a few intelligent indigenous people have been shown in this research paper on how important is the contribution of these great tribal figures in the formation of present India. The results of the study revealed that the culture and practices of the tribes of India form a rich part of our history. Whether it is in the realm of arts, music, dance, handicrafts, or innovation, their way of life is one that is unique. However, they are oppressed and ostracized in various ways. But that has not stopped them from making a mark in mainstream India with their contributions to the economy, sports, politics, and much more!

*Keywords:*Tribe, Contribution, India, Tribal talent, Indigenous.

1. Introduction

Indian society is divided into tribal, rural, and urban societies according to geographical context and sociocultural traits. An essential component of Indian society is the tribal groups. There are tribes in practically every region of the world. India has the second-largest number of tribal people after Africa. The diverse tribal population of India, which has a diversity of environments, shows a rich cultural mosaic. The tribal population is mostly isolated and inhabits steep woodlands or clearly defined regions with their own unique culture, language, religion, and a strong sense of morality. Tribals are recognized as the first settlers on the Indian Peninsula and are known to be native landowners. Indian tribal people are often referred to as Adivasis (original inhabitants). They are seen as being socioeconomically backward in the modern world. Indian tribes are studied by anthropologists and sociologists in light of their unique demographic, ecological, economic, political, historical, and sociocultural environments. Few indigenous tribes live on plains, and the majority of them are situated in forests, plateaus, or hills in physically remote areas of India. The majority of them continue to engage in shifting or established agriculture, as well as being pastoralists, craftsmen, and laborers, among other means of subsistence (Ramesh Thapar: 1996). A significant portion of our history is shaped by the customs and culture of the Indian tribes. Their way of life is distinctive, whether it is in the fields of the arts, music, dancing, handicrafts, or innovation. They do, however, often slip under the mainstream Indians' notice. They have nevertheless made significant contributions to the economy, politics, technology, sports, and much more, leaving their stamp on the majority of India.

2. Literature Review

Olympic gold medalist and American athlete James Francis Thorpe (Sac and Fox Indian) was from the United States. Thorpe, a member of the Sac and Fox Nation, became the first American Indian to win an Olympic gold medal for his country. He won two Olympic gold medals at the 1912 Summer Games and was one of the most versatile athletes in modern sports (one in classic pentathlon and the other in decathlon). He also played both university and professional American football, basketball, and professional baseball. Thorpe served as the American Professional Football Association's (later the NFL) official first president from 1920 to 1921. (Zindars, 2015)

Sacheen Cruz Littlefeather was an American model, actress, and Native American civil right activist. She was the first indigenous woman and woman of colour to utilize the Academy Awards stage to express her political views. She is now one of the elders passing information down through the generations.(Rose, 2021)

A well-known New Zealand politician, Apirana Turupa Ngata (July 3, 1874 - July 14, 1950), is renowned for his efforts in promoting and defending Maori culture and language and has often been referred to as the most prominent Maori politician to have served in Parliament in the middle of the 20th century. His image is on the fifty-dollar note, establishing his reputation as one of the most notable any leader of New Zealand throughout the 20th century. Ngata worked as a lawyer before entering politics in 1897, when he founded the Young Maori Party with several Te Aute College alumni, including future cabinet member Maui Pomare. He was chosen as the Liberal Member of Parliament (MP) for Eastern Maori in 1905 and held this position for over 40 years. From 1928 until 1934, he worked for the Government as the Minister of Native Affairs. Although he was forced to quit as a minister due to a publicly reported spending scandal, he endeavored to implement as many changes for Mori as he could in this Nevertheless, and he remained the MP for Eastern Maori until 1943, when he was defeated by Tiaki Omana, a Ratana candidate who was a supporter of Labour when Labour swept the Maori electorates.(Stafford & Williams, 2008)

Filmmaker, an actor, and comedian Taika David Cohen ONZM, better known by his stage as Taika Waititi, was born in New Zealand on August 16, 1975. He has received awards such as an Academy Award, a BAFTA Award, a Grammy Award, and other recognition in addition to two Primetime Emmy nominations. The highest-grossing New Zealand films in 2010 and 2016, respectively were his full-length works Boy (2010) and Hunt for the Wilderpeople. He received a nomination for the Academy Award for Best Live Action Short Film for his 2003 short film Two Cars, One Night. He has most recently worked as a filmmaker on the superhero films Thor: Ragnarok (2017) and Thor: Love and Thunder (2022), as well as the dark comedy Jojo Rabbit (2019), in which he also created and performed as a fictional Adolf Hitler. Jojo Rabbit had six nominations for Academy Awards and won the Best Adapted Screenplay award. Waititi also won a Grammy for creating the music for the movie. Two television comedies that Waititi co-created and executive produced are Reservation Dogs, and Our Flag Means Death. Additionally, he executive produced and directed the dramedy series Reservation Dogs. (Geary, 2012)

Neville Thomas Bonner AO was an Australian politician and the first Aboriginal Australian to be elected to the Australian Parliament (March 28, 1922–February 5, 1999). The Queensland Parliament chose him to fill a casual vacancy in the state's Senate representation, and he subsequently became the first Indigenous Australian to be chosen by the people to serve in the legislature. After resigning from the party in 1983, Neville Bonner continued to be a strong advocate for Indigenous rights until his death in 1999.(NAA, n.d)

3. Methodology

1. *Data Collection Method*

There are so many talented indigenous scientists, engineers, sports persons, activists, teachers, and other geniuses in this country; among them, 40 tribal geniuses were randomly selected for the present study. The study took into account qualitative factors. The research article examined and analyzed a few case studies of a few indigenous geniuses. The study mostly focuses on secondary data.

2. *Secondary Data*

Secondary data was used for the review of the literature and the development of the research. For secondary data, we explored Google, e-books, media stories, online journals, research sites, etc.

4. Objectives

I. To highlight the contribution of tribal talent in India's leading development sectors
II. To encourage tribal people to contribute to the development of the country

Table 1 Indigenous people under consideration

Sl. No	Name	Sex	Profession	Source
1	Droupadi Murmu	Female	President Of India	https://en.wikipedia.org/wiki/Droupadi_Murmu
2	Hemant Saren	Male	Chief Minister of Jharkhand	https://en.wikipedia.org/wiki/Hemant_Soren
3	Dhananjay Hembram	Male	Jt. Secretary at Odisha Govt	https://www.facebook.com/dhananjay.hembram/
4	Jaipal Singh Munda	Male	Politician, Prolific Writer, And A Fine Sportsman	https://en.wikipedia.org/wiki/Jaipal_Singh_Munda
5	Chandrani Murmu	Female	Politician	https://en.wikipedia.org/wiki/Chandrani_Murmu
6	Rukmini Devi	Female	Politician	https://www.shethepeople.tv/home-top-video/tribal-woman-sarpanch-rukmini-devi/
7	Bhaichung Bhutia	Male	Footballer	https://en.wikipedia.org/wiki/Bhaichung_Bhutia
8	Mary Kom	Female	Boxer	https://en.wikipedia.org/wiki/Mary_Kom
9	Elizabeth Beck	Female	Cyclist	https://www.shethepeople.tv/shesport/who-is-elizabeth-beck-national-games/
10	Komalika Bari	Female	Archer	https://www.shethepeople.tv/shestars/who-is-komalika-bari-archer-in-finals-of-world-archery-youth-championship/
11	Dilip Tirkey	Male	Ex-Captain of The Then Indian Hockey Team	https://en.m.wikipedia.org/wiki/Dilip_Tirkey
12	Birendra Lakra	Male	Hockey Player	https://en.wikipedia.org/wiki/Birendra_Lakra
13	Abhimanyu Mallick	Male	Scientist	https://odishabytes.com/odisha-youth-trudges-from-tribal-village-to-become-isro-scientist/
14	Sukram Baberia	Male	IIT Kharagpur Student	https://www.google.com/amp/s/thelogicalindian.com/amp/uplifting/mason-couples-son-gets-admission-in-iit-29609
15	M Krishnadas	Male	MTech Degree from IIT Palakkad.	https://timesofindia.indiatimes.com/city/kochi/kerala-m-krishnadas-is-first-tribal-student-from-palakkad-to-get-an-mtech-from-iit/articleshow/91975162.cms
16	Savitri Kashyap	Female	Engineer	https://www.indiatoday.in/education-today/news/story/tribal-girl-chattisgarh-15133-2016-06-20
17	Tulasi Gowda	Female	Indian Environmentalist	https://en.wikipedia.org/wiki/Tulsi_Gowda
18	Tulasi Munda	Female	Social Activist	https://en.wikipedia.org/wiki/Tulasi_Munda
19	Soni Sori	Female	Tribal Rights Activist and A School Teacher	https://en.wikipedia.org/wiki/Soni_Sori
20	Gyarishi Devi	Female	Activist	https://feminisminindia.com/2019/12/11/faces-indias-adivasi-tribal-activism/
21	Jamuna Tudu	Female	Environmental Activist	https://en.wikipedia.org/wiki/Jamuna_Tudu
22	Gladson Dungdung	Male	Human Rights Activist	https://en.wikipedia.org/wiki/Gladson_Dungdung
23	Kamala Pujari	Female	Promoting Organic Farming	https://en.wikipedia.org/wiki/Kamala_Pujari
24	Lakshmikutty	Female	Traditional Medicine.	https://en.wikipedia.org/wiki/Lakshmikutty
25	Padala Bhudevi	Female	Working With Widows and Tribal Women	https://en.wikipedia.org/wiki/Padala_Bhudevi
26	Dr. Shila Elezabeth Besra	Female	Principal, Technical Officer	https://iicb.res.in/faculty/shila-elizabeth-besra
27	Alok Sagar	Male	Ex-IIT Delhi Professor	https://dishabharat.org/prof-alok-sagar-messiah-for-the-tribals/
28	Ayan Kumar Tudu	Male	Asst. Professor	http://www.jaduniv.edu.in/profile.php?uid=986
29	Bharati Tudu	Female	Asst. Professor	http://www.jaduniv.edu.in/profile.php?uid=840
30	Bipan Tudu	Male	Professor	http://www.jaduniv.edu.in/profile.php?uid=407
31	Bhimsen Tudu	Male	Asst. Professor	http://www.jaduniv.edu.in/profile.php?uid=799
32	Babulal Tudu	Male	Lab Attendant	
33	Dr. Kanchu Charan Mahali	Male	Former IPS Officer	https://university.kiss.ac.in/profiles/dr-kanhu-charan-mahali-ips-retd/
34	Sreedhanya Suresh	Female	IAS Officer	https://byjus.com/free-ias-prep/sreedhanya-suresh-upsc-result-2018/
35	Dr. Damayanti Besra	Female	Santali Writer	http://sahitya-akademi.gov.in/library/meettheauthor/damayanti_beshra.pdf
36	Ruby Hembrom	Female	Indigenous Cultural Practitioner, Documentarian, Writer and Publisher	https://afsee.atlanticfellows.org/ruby-hembrom
37	Dayamani Barla	Female	Journalist And Activist	https://en.wikipedia.org/wiki/Dayamani_Barla
38	Anupriya Madhumita Lakra	Female	Pilot	https://www.shethepeople.tv/news/anupriya-madhumita-lakra-first-tribal-woman-pilot/
39	Lipsa Hembram	Female	Fashion Designer	https://www.theweek.in/leisure/lifestyle/2020/11/27/how-lipsa-hembram-is-modernizing-santali-sarees.html
40	Riya Tirkey	Female	Model	https://beautypageants.indiatimes.com/miss-india/miss-india-contestants/2022/riya-tirkey/contestantprofile/92029598.cms

5. Indigenous People of India

5.1. Indigenous Politicians of India

The tribal society has developed a distinct identity inside the nation. The tribal community has made its own place by following the duty towards society. This society has played a major role in saving water, forest, and land. Recently, India got its first tribal President from the Santhal community, one of India's Scheduled Tribes, constituting less than ten percent of the population.

Case Study 1

Name-Droupadi Murmu

Age-64 years

Sex- Female

Marital Status- Widow

Droupadi Murmu was born to a Santali family on June 20, 1958, in Uparbeda village within the Baidaposi area of Rairangpur, Odisha. At the local primary school in Uparbeda, Murmu studied primary education. She came to Bhubaneswar at the age of 5 to pursue higher education. Her father, Biranchi Narayan Tudu, was a farmer. Indian politician Droupadi Murmu has served as the nation's 15th and current President since July 25, 2022. She is the second woman to occupy the position after Pratibha Patil and the first member of a tribal group to do so.

Additionally, she is also the youngest President in history. She held a variety of positions in the cabinet of the Government of Odisha between 2000 and 2004 before being elected President. Between 2015 through 2021, she served as Jharkhand's ninth governor.(Wikipedia contributors, 2022e)

Case Study 2

Name-Hemant Soren

Age-47 years

Sex- Male

Marital Status- Married

Hemant Soren was born on August 10, 1975, in Nemara, Ramgarh District, Bihar (now Jharkhand). He belongs to the Santal Community. He completed his education at Patna High School in Patna, Bihar. He studied Mechanical Engineering in Ranchi, Jharkhand's Birla Institute of Technology, after completing his 12th-grade coursework. He didn't, however, finish his college degree. From June 2009 until January 2010, he served in the Rajya Sabha. In 2009, he began his political career as a Legislative Assembly (MLA) Member. Later, from 2010 to 2013, he served as deputy chief minister of Jharkhand. He is the leader of the Jharkhand Mukti Morcha, a political party in Jharkhand. He took his oath as Jharkhand's 11th chief minister on December 29, 2019.(Wikipedia contributors, 2022b)

5.2. *Indigenous Environmentalist of India*

Before chemical medicines were introduced to India, there was herbal medicine that was produced from the environment. It is well known that tribal people have been using traditional medicines since the time of their ancestors, and many of us in the contemporary world have started to admire them.

Case Study 3

Name-Tulsi Gowda

Age-78 years

Sex- Female

Marital Status- Married

Tulsi Gowda is an Indian environmentalist. She was born in 1944 into a tribal family of the Halakki tribe in the Honnalli village. This community is situated in the Uttara Kannada region of the Indian state of Karnataka and lies in between a rural and urban setting. Gowda was born into a low-income family and lost her father when she was only two years old. When she was old enough, she was forced to work as a day labourer at a neighbouring nursery. She never attended school or picked up reading. She maintains the Forest Department's nurseries and has planted more than 30,000 trees. The Indian Government and various organisations have recognised her contributions. She received the fourth-highest civilian honour in India, the Padma Shri, from the Government in 2021. Because of her aptitude for identifying the mother tree of any kind of tree, she is known as the "Encyclopedia of the Forest."(Wikipedia contributors, 2022a)

Apart from them, Jamuna Tudu, an Indian environmental activist from Jharkhand; Gladson Dungdung, a human rights activist writer, and founder of the Adivasi Publications of Jharkhand; Soni Sori, a 41-year-old tribal rights activist, has been a fearless and vocal critic of police violence and brutality towards tribals in the state of Chhattisgarh are a few indigenous activists of India have fought against external forces, defending their forests and rights over land.

5.3. *Indigenous Social Activist of India*

We cannot ignore the fact that indigenous people in India are fighting for their rights to the forests and their land. Extremist capitalism and pseudo-development techniques are to blame for the discrimination that tribes experience over their rights to their lands and forests. Many activists have fought against outside influences to protect their woods and land rights. Check out some of the fresh faces in tribal activism!

Case Study 4

Name-Tulasi Munda

Age-75 years

Sex- Female

Social activist Tulasi Munda is from the Indian state of Odisha. On July 15, 1947, Munda was born in the Odisha hamlet of Kainshi, which is now a part of the Keonjhar district. She is uneducated and has no formal schooling. She is an Adivasi of the Munda ethnic group. To prevent the local Adivasi population's children from becoming child labourers in the mines, Munda established an informal school there in 1964. She herself had worked as a child labourer in the mines of Keonjhar. She received the Padma Shri honour from the Indian Government in 2001 for her work promoting literacy among the underprivileged Adivasi people of Odisha. She is often known as "Tulasi Apa," literally meaning "Sister Tulasi" in Odia.(Wikipedia contributors, 2021)

5.4. *Indigenous IITians of India*

It is out of the question to think of IITs for the sons and daughters of auto drivers, masons, roadside tea vendors, landless labourers, security guards, daily wage labourers, taxi drivers, and housemaids from tribal communities. But some tribal students achieved it by working hard in their studies.

Case Study 5

Name-Sukram Baberia

Age- 22 years

Sex- Male

Marital Status- Single

Sukram Baberia comes from a tribal village in the Indian state of Gujarat's Dahod District. Baberia was raised in a setting where pursuing higher education was difficult. He used to assist his parents, who are masons, on Ahmedabad building sites by lifting bricks. He attended a grant-in-aid school until he was in class 10, after which he attended a government school until he was in class 8. After that, he was accepted into Dahod's state-run Adarsh Residential School. According to The Times of India, Sukram enrolled himself at the Aspee Shakilam Biotechnology Institute at the Navsari Agriculture University in Surat for advanced education in 2017. India's poor youth often find it tough to pursue higher education. But Sukram Baberia overcame all obstacles to get a decent education, and now he has also been offered a spot at one of the nation's most esteemed institutions, IIT Kharagpur.(Nazir, 2021)

Case Study 6

Name-Alok Sagar

Age- 72 Years

Sex- Male

Former IIT Delhi professor Alok Sagar quit his well-paying position in 1982 to help tribal people, support women's equality, and maintain a connection to the natural world. Sagar has a Ph.D. from Houston University in Texas, the US, and graduation and master's degrees from IIT Delhi. He tutored Raghuram Rajan, a former governor of the RBI. However, he felt that none of these degrees mattered, and in one of Madhya Pradesh's most isolated regions, he discovered his real calling. Sagar has lived in Kochamu for the last 26 years; it is an area without electricity or roads. He has been teaching others how to cultivate trees and care for the environment since he is passionate about nature.(Disha Bharat, 2018)

A few other names include Savitri Kashyap, a tribal girl who conquered all challenges and passed one of the country's most difficult examinations, the IITJEE. The first tribal person from the area to get an MTech degree from IIT-Palakkad is M Krishnadas, a tribal student from the isolated Kalkandiyur tribal village of Kottathara near Attapadi on the border between Tamil Nadu and Kerala.

5.5. *Indigenous Sports Persons of India*

The Indian tribes are well-known for their natural stamina and strength, which is a product of their lifestyle. As a result, several well-known sports personalities are descended from Indian tribes. Some of them are discussed below:

Case Study 7

Name-Bhaichung Bhutia

Age-45 years

Sex- Male

Marital Status- Married

In an agricultural family, Bhaichung Bhutia was born on December 15, 1976, in Tinkitam, Sikkim, India. He was a striker and a former professional footballer from India. He began his studies at St. Xavier's School in Pakyong, East Sikkim. He received a football scholarship from SAI at nine, allowing him to attend the Tashi Namgyal Academy in Gangtok. Bhutia dropped out of school in 1993 at sixteen to play professionally for Kolkata's East Bengal

FC Bhutia is regarded as carrying the Indian football flag in the international sphere. I. M. Vijayan, a three-time winner of the Indian Player of the Year award, called Bhutia God's gift to Indian football.(Wikipedia contributors, 2022d)

Case Study 8

Name-Mangte Chungneijang Mary Kom

Age-39 years

Sex- Female

Marital Status- Married

Mangte Chungneijang Mary Kom was born on November 24, 1982, in the Indian state of rural Manipur's Kagathei village, Moirang Lamkhai. She is a politician, former Rajya Sabha member, and amateur boxer from India. Kom participated in football, volleyball, and other sports at his school. She decided to switch from athletics to boxing in 2000, and Dingko Singh's accomplishments served as her motivation. The first boxer (male or female) to have won eight medals at a World Championship, the first female boxer to have earned a medal at each of the first seven World Championships, and the only boxer to have won six World Amateur Boxing Championship championships. She is the first female boxer from India to have earned a spot in the 2012 Summer Olympics, when she competed at flyweight (51 kg) and took home a bronze medal. She was also recognised as the top female light flyweight in the world by the Amateur International Boxing Association (AIBA). She won a gold medal in the Asian Games in 2014 in Incheon, South Korea, making history as the first Indian female boxer to do so. The 2018 Commonwealth Games saw her win a gold medal as well. She also holds the record for having won the Asian Amateur Boxing Champion title a record six times, making her the only boxer to do so. Mary Kom won the 51 kg gold medal in the President's Cup in Indonesia.(Wikipedia contributors, 2022c)

Dilip Tirkey, an Odisha native of the Oraon tribe, was once regarded as one of the world's toughest hockey defenders to defeat and a force to be reckoned with on the pitch. The finest cyclist in the state, Elizabeth Beck, a 28-year-old tribal woman from Chattisgarh, showed herself and was chosen for the National Games. In contrast, Komalika Bari, India's second female archer, recently won the gold medal in the women's cadet recurve category at the World Archery Youth Championships in Madri as a result of her perseverance and willpower. These are only a handful of the many individuals of tribal descent who have achieved greatness in sports and brought honour to India!

5.6. *Indigenous Government Officer of India*

Today, tribal people not only attend classes, dress well, and send their kids to school, but they also enrol for the Civil Services exam in hopes of passing and becoming IAS officers. No matter how particular backward tribes were when the country gained its independence, they are now educated and actively participate in the country's development.

Case Study 9

Name-Kanhu Charan Mahali

Sex- Male

Marital Status- Married

Dr. Kanhu Charan Mahali is a native of the Mayurbhanj district of Odisha. He formerly held the Additional Director General of Police position and was an IPS officer from the Tamilnadu cadre. Before that, he worked for the Madhya Pradesh cadre of the Indian Forest Service (IFS). He is an effective administrator with 34 years of extensive and diverse experience in the State Government of India and the Government of India. In New Delhi and Bhubaneswar, he also held the position of Assistant Director for the Intelligence Bureau (IB). He graduated with an M.Sc. (Ag) in Agricultural Economics from the Orissa University of Agriculture and Technology (OUAT), Bhubaneswar, and a Ph.D. from the University of Madras.(Kalinga Institute of Social Science, 2022)

Case Study 10

Name-Sreedhanya Suresh

Age- 26

Sex- Female

Marital Status- Unmarried

Sreedhanya Suresh is a member of the Wayanad tribe of the Kurichiya people of Kerala. She proved herself and became the first tribal woman from Kerala to pass the Civil Services Examination administered by the Union Public Service Commission, India, in spite of all the challenges and destitution. In the 2018 UPSC Civil Services Examination, she earned an all-India rank of 410.(Das, 2020)

6. Discussion

A tribe is an endogamous human social group that lives in a particular environment, has its own set of rituals, and has a variety of distinctive characteristics, such as its dialect, folklore, and cultural aspects of clothing, instruments, habitats, artifacts, and music. Tribes are often isolated from the outside world. They differ from other politically significant and numerically bigger populations because of their strong historical ties to a particular place and their cultural and historical uniqueness. They are dispersed across the nation and live in hilly and forested areas. Because they can get everything they need on their land and don't want to interact with the dominant population, they have spent much time alone over the years. As a result, their education levels, way of life, and skill sets lag behind those of the dominant populations. They are then labelled as being primitive and outdated due to this.

Despite several government initiatives to develop the community members, tribal communities throughout the nation are notorious for their backwardness. However, some tribe members succeeded by studying hard.

India is known for its many religions and vibrant culture. The Indian government has worked on behalf of tribals from time to time, and the results are now visible.Within the country, the tribal civilization has established a distinct identity. The tribal community developed itself by fulfilling its social responsibilities. This society has made a substantial contribution to the protection of the land, water, and forests.The job of integrating tribal people into society was particularly challenging due to the diverse living situations that tribal people experience across the nation, as well as their unique languages and customs. In the 2011 census, more than 600 tribal communities with a combined population of around 104 million people—or roughly 8.6% of all Indians—were counted. The largest concentrations are found in Madhya Pradesh, Bihar, Orissa, north-eastern India, West Bengal, Maharashtra, Gujarat, and Rajasthan. They mostly resided in the hills and woods of colonial India, where they were quite isolated and had traditions, customs, cultures, and ways of life that were very distinct from those of their non-tribal neighbors.

- In most regions of the nation, colonialism compelled tribals to undergo drastic modifications as market pressures destroyed their relative seclusion, and they were integrated with British and princely administrations.

- A huge number of moneylenders, merchants, revenue farmers, and other middlemen and minor officials infiltrated tribal lands, destroying the tribals' traditional way of life. They were relegated to the condition of agricultural workers, sharecroppers, and rack-rented tenants as a result of their increasing financial burden and the loss of their land to outsiders.

- A large number of people were compelled to retreat further into the hills. Late-enacted legislation to prevent tribal land alienation was unsuccessful in stopping the process.

- At the same time, "missionaries were destroying their art, dances, weaving, and whole culture." Colonialism also changed the tribal people's connection to the forest. The forest provided them with raw materials for their handicrafts, food, firewood, and cattle feed. In many areas of India, the desire for land on the side of emigrant peasants from the plains resulted in the destruction of forests, depriving tribals of their traditional means of survival. Colonial authorities implemented forest regulations that prohibited shifting cultivation and severely limited tribals' usage of the forest and access to forest goods in order to safeguard forests and enable their commercial use.

- In the nineteenth and twentieth centuries, a number of tribal uprisings, including the Santhal revolt and the Munda rebellion led by Birsa Munda, as well as the involvement of tribal people, were caused by land loss, debt, middleman exploitation, denial of access to forests and forest products, and oppression and extortion by police, forest officials, and other government officials.

The above comments clearly show that the tribal people suffered a lot from the non-tribal community. Therefore, during the 19th and 20th centuries AD, a lot of uprisings and rebellions were triggered by the sufferings of tribal people, mainly the non-tribal—for instance, the Santhal and Munda uprisings.

The preservation of the rich and unique culture of the tribal people who live in different areas of India, however, received a lot of attention when India became an independent nation.The tribal tribes in India have grown to be who they are in close vicinity to the natural resources that have shaped their social structures, religious beliefs, economic systems, and modes of production. They have established a symbiotic relationship with their immediate surroundings throughout time. For them, land represents their cultural identity and life rather than just being a means of subsistence.

As we have seen in the discussion above, the tribals are getting out of their ruts, getting a higher education, and progress. For example, from case studies, we understand that many tribal faces have gained prominence in present-day India despite facing various life difficulties. Recently, India got its first tribal President from the Santhal community, one of India's Scheduled Tribes. It is a great achievement and a proud moment for the entire tribal community and the country. Today, the remarkable role of tribals in moving India forward is clear in front of our eyes, and we cannot deny this.

7. Conclusion

From the above discussion, we can understand that Indian tribals have improved a lot. The Indian Government has made a special contribution to make the tribals reach this level of progress today. Framers of the Indian Constitution realized that certain marginalized sections in India were excluded from the national mainstream and suffered extremely from social, educational, and economic backwardness. They considered that this section needed special constitutional safeguards to protect their rights and interests to enable them to join the national mainstream. The Indian Constitution provides protection and safeguards for Scheduled Tribes to promote their educational and economic interests. The Government has made consistent efforts for their development which is obvious from the Five-Year Plans. The Government takes special developmental programs and protective measures to augment the pace of tribal development. A nation's development is directly related to the accessibility and opportunities to avail educational facilities to the people. And it has always been a great challenge for the Government to provide education to all tribal people. The Government has been seriously improving its educational standards through various programs and schemes. Some of the programs and schemes launched for the promotion of education among Indian tribal people are the Post-Matric Scholarship Scheme, Hostel for ST students' girls' and boys', Rajiv Gandhi National Fellowship Scheme (RGNF), Ashram School in Tribal Sub-Plan Area, Ashram School in Tribal Sub-Plan Area, Book Bank, etc.

Despite constitutional provisions and safeguards with various government initiatives and programs, educating tribal children is still a major concern for the Government. There are so many sociocultural, economic, and geographical, for why the literacy rate of tribal people has never been at par with the entire population, and the gap between them is always high. All over the country, tribals still face various educational problems, In most of the states, official/regional languages are used for classroom teaching, and these are not understood by the tribal children at the primary level; most of the schools located in tribal areas have minimal infrastructural facilities; most of the tribal areas are hilly, and the road facilities are inadequate, so the child faces transport problems to reach school; in tribal areas, most of the schools don't provide basic amenities such as toilets, drinking water, electricity and adequate classroom for proper teaching, etc. The Indian Government should find a way to solve these problems soon. Then the tribals can contribute much better to the development of our country.

Recommendations

- In tribal areas, schools should be appointed local area teachers and female teachers also in school.
- Teaching and learning should be imparted in the local language.
- The Government should take some specific initiative through various programs like awareness camps, street drama, counseling, etc., which can create awareness among the tribals about the importance of education.
- In tribal area problem of transport prevail; to overcome this, there should be residential schools.
- Relevant study material in the local language should be used to teach tribal students.
- Tribal area schools should have various extracurricular activities along with studies.

References

Das, R. (2020, June 15). *Sreedhanya Suresh, Kerala's First Woman Tribal IAS Officer, Is Now Asst Collector Of Kozhikode.* She The People. https://www.shethepeople.tv/news/sreedhanya-suresh-kerala-first-woman-tribal-ias-officer-is-now-asst-collector-of-kozhikode/

Disha Bharat. (2018, October 7). *Prof.Alok Sagar- Messiah for the Tribals.* Disha Bharat. https://dishabharat.org/prof-alok-sagar-messiah-for-the-tribals/

Geary, D. (2012). Taika Waititi-Boy Wonder! *New Zealand Journal of Media Studies, 13*(1), 14–27.

Kalinga Institute of Social Science. (2022, February 16). *Dr. Kanhu Charan Mahali, IPS (Retd.).* Kalinga Institute of Social Science.

NAA. (n.d.). *Indigenous leader and Senator (1922–99).* National Archives of Australia. Retrieved October 1, 2022, from https://www.naa.gov.au/explore-collection/first-australians/other-resources-about-first-australians/neville-bonner

Nazir, T. (2021, July 21). *Mason Couple's Son Aims Big, Gets Admission in IIT .* The Logical Indian. https://thelogicalindian.com/uplifting/mason-couples-son-gets-admission-in-iit-29609

Rose, S. (2021). Sacheen Littlefeather. In *The Guardian.*

Stafford, J., & Williams, M. (2008). Apirana Turupa Ngata, 1874 – 1950. In *Kōtare* (Vol. 7, Issue 2).

Wikipedia contributors. (2021, July 31). *Tulasi Munda.* Wikipedia, The Free Encyclopedia. https://en.wikipedia.org/w/index.php?title=Tulasi_Munda&oldid=1036466337

Wikipedia contributors. (2022a, September 27). *Tulsi Gowda.* Wikipedia, The Free Encyclopedia. https://en.wikipedia.org/w/index.php?title=Tulsi_Gowda&oldid=1111547682

Wikipedia contributors. (2022b, October 3). *Hemant Soren.* Wikipedia, The Free Encyclopedia. https://en.wikipedia.org/w/index.php?title=Hemant_Soren&oldid=1113777068

Wikipedia contributors. (2022c, October 7). *Mary Kom.* Wikipedia, The Free Encyclopedia. https://en.wikipedia.org/w/index.php?title=Mary_Kom&oldid=1114570487

Wikipedia contributors. (2022d, October 20). *Bhaichung Bhutia.* Wikipedia, The Free Encyclopedia. https://en.wikipedia.org/w/index.php?title=Bhaichung_Bhutia&oldid=1117208984

Wikipedia contributors. (2022e, October 21). *Droupadi Murmu.* Wikipedia, The Free Encyclopedia. https://en.wikipedia.org/w/index.php?title=Droupadi_Murmu&oldid=1117340278

Zindars, M. C. (2015). *A with Honors Projects* (Vol. 148). http://spark.parkland.edu/ah/148

CHAPTER THREE

Tribal Education in India

Dr. Savita Mishra: Principal, Vidyasaagar College of Education, Phansidewa, Darjeeling, West Bengal, India

Introduction

Education, especially in its elementary form, is considered of utmost importance to the tribals because it's crucial for total development of tribal communities and is particularly helpful to build confidence among the tribes to deal with outsiders on equal terms. Despite the sincere and concerted efforts by the government for the overall development of the scheduled tribes, they are still far behind in almost all the standard parameters of development. They are not able to participate in the process of development, as they are not aware of most of the progrmmes and policies made for their upliftment. This is mainly due to the high incidence of illiteracy and very low level of education among the tribal people. Hence, the educational status of the scheduled tribes and the role of governance in this direction are highly essential. It is well known that the educational background of tribes is very discouraging as compared to the rest of the population. So, education is an important avenue for upgrading the economic and social conditions of the Scheduled Tribes. In this context, the objective of this paper is to analyse the trend of literacy rate, gross enrolment ratio, dropout rates and Gender Parity Index of tribal education in India.

Development should not be studied in isolation. Development is not synonymous with the growth of a few affluent persons. As Amartya Sen (1999) stated unless the capabilities among human beings are adequately addressed and deprivations faced by marginalized groups are overcome, development cannot take place. In fact he stressed on the capabilities and human freedoms, and this freedom can only be achieved when the people are guaranteed political freedom, economic facilities, social opportunities, transparency, and security. Although these conditions are different from one another, they are all inter-connected.

Problems of Tribal Education:

There are many critical issues and problems in the field of tribal education. They are as follows:

1. **Medium of language:** Language is one of the important constraints of tribal children which prevents them access to education.
2. **The Location of the Village:** The physical barrier creates a hindrance for the children of a tribal village to attend the school in a neighboring village.
3. **Economic Condition:** The economic condition of tribal people is so poor that they do not desire to spare their children or their labour power and allow them to attend schools.

4. **Attitude of the parents:** As education does not yield any immediate economic return, the tribal parents prefer to engage their children in remunerative employment which supplements the family income.

5. **Teacher Related Problems:** In the remote tribal areas the teacher absenteeism is a regular phenomenon and this affects largely the quality of education.
6. **Lack of Proper monitoring:** Proper monitoring is hindered by poor coordination between the Tribal Welfare Department and School Education Department.

Challenging Issues of Tribal Education:

Our constitution has many provisions and safeguards of the tribal, beside government taken lot of policy programmes to develop the educational, economic and social conditions of the Tribes but today it is unable to reach the sustainable goal. In recent the educational status of tribal children is very important issues to the government. Many times in the government reposts mention lot of obstacle to tribal education in India that make more challenge of the tribals. Many times in the government reports mention lot of obstacles to tribal education in India that make more challenge to education of the tribals. The important contemporary socio-economic and cultural challenging issues of tribal education faced by tribal people are mentions bellow:

1. Economic Challenge:

Today the Indian tribes are facing poor economic conditions and unable to proper daily life with basic need. In these socio-economic contestation the tribal parents are don't send the children to school for education. Economic challenge is an important issue to Indian They send their children to various work for the money for better livelihood.

2. Infrastructural Challenge:

An infrastructure is the basic condition to any development related idea. Maximum school of the tribal areas have not sufficient infrastructural facilities. In this school are not decorated with teaching learning materials, study materials, sanitary systems etc has not maintained. Due to problems of the infrastructural facilities tribal children are not attracted in the school premises. So the infrastructural outcome has made more dropout student of the tribal community.

3. Unwillingness of Parents on Education:

The parents of tribal community are unawareness and illiterate towards education. On the other hand tribal community is not agreeing sending their children to the school. So the parents are not encouraged to the pupils to continue the study. Beside the tribal parents are not allow to send their girls along to the school specially co-ed school.

4. Language related Challenge:

Language related barriers are the important challenges to tribal education in India. Every tribal groups has own mother tong and in the residence they talk in to own community with their own mother tong. Maximum Indian states or union territory are used regional languages for classroom teaching at the primary level. The tribal students do not understand this language. The study materials are prepared by official language of the state, the tribal students understands as a foreign language.

5. Geographical Challenge:

The Maximum tribal groups are living in hilly and forest areas and these areas geographically unfavourable towards modern education facility. The tribal inhabited areas located away from modern civilization and modern opportunities due this reason in this area do not benefited by the modern educational opportunities.

6. Teacher related Challenge:

The teachers play an important role in Indian traditional education system. Most of the tribal areas school has a problem regarding regularity in school of the teacher. Due this problem make distance between tribal students and teacher that deprived the tribal student. Maximum time the tribal society has neglected by maximum teachers, so it is not possible to provide education through proper way of the tribal students as like as general students.

7. Proper Monitoring Challenge:

Lack of proper monitoring make more challenge to the tribal education of India. Any development policy and programme can't achieve the proper goal without proper monitoring system. Our government take many policies and programme to develop the educational status of scheduled tribes but there have lack of proper monitoring. Maximum time tribal development department and school education department has not maintaining the proper monitoring systems on tribal education.

Government Policies and Programmes for Tribal Education:

Starting from the First Five Year Plan Period1 (1951-1956) the government is steadily allocating financial resources for the purpose of tribal development. Towards, the end of the plan (1954), 43 Special Multipurpose Tribal Development Projects (MTDPs) were created. During the Third Five Year Plan Period (1961-1966), the government of India adopted the strategy of converting areas with more than 66 per cent tribal concentration into Tribal Development Blocks (TBDs). By the end of Fourth Five Year Plan (1969-1974), the number of TBDs in the country rose to 504. Additionally, in 1972 the Tribal Sub-Plan Strategy (TSP) was implemented by the Ministry of Education and Social Welfare. TSP was based on twin objectives of socio-economic development and protection against exploitation. It was generally implemented in the areas where the

Scheduled Tribe population was more than 50 per cent of the total population.

The PESA (The Panchayats Extension to Scheduled Areas) Act, 1996 in fact, has made it mandatory for the States having scheduled areas to make specific provisions for giving wide-ranging powers to the tribes on the matters relating to decision-making and development of their community. A centrally-sponsored government scheme of ashram schools exclusively for ST children from elementary to higher secondary levels was initiated in the 1970s. But the poor quality of education in ashram schools, however, has undermined confidence in education as a vehicle for social mobility.

The Janshala Programme is a collaborative effort of the Government of India (GOI) and five UN Agencies –UNDP, UNICEF, UNESCO, ILO and UNFPA –a community based primary education programme, aims to make primary education more accessible and effective, especially for girls and children in deprived communities, marginalised groups, Scheduled Caste/ Scheduled Tribes/minorities, children with specific needs.

After independence government of India has been trying to develop the socio-economic and educational conditions of the tribes through lat of government sponsored programs and policies. The important government initiatives for the tribal education are mentioned below:

A. Various Committees/Commissions Related to Tribal Development:

The government of India is trying to all round development of tribal's by implementation of recommendation from various committees. Formation the important committees regarding tribal development at difference time by the government of India and made effective their recommendation like, Elwin Committee, Dhebar Commission, Lokur Committee, Bhuria Committee, Mungekar Committee, Virginius Xaxa Committee etc.

B. Literacy Mission:

In the year 1978, Adult Education Scheme was launched at national level. In this programme, attempts were made to make the people literate in the age group of 15 to 35 years. Although a favourable environment was created by this programme towards literacy, but desired success was not achieved. In the year 1988, national literacy mission programme was established. In this programme, centre-based system of education was changed to time-bound region-based system. Voluntary organisations were attached to this programme. In this programme, all illiterates in the age group of 15 to 45 years were covered. For non-enrolled and drop outs, Informal Education programme was introduced.

C. Informal Education Programme:

There are many villages in our country where there is no school. In order to provide primary education facilities in those villages, informal education programme has been implemented. The Government has started special educational centres in those areas to provide primary level education.

D. Scholarship for Tribal Student:

For the children of STs SCs and backward classes, scholarship is provided to continue their education. At Block level, Block Scholarship committee is created. On the recommendations of these committees, the children studying in Class-I to Class-X receive scholarship. On the other hand Students of SCs and STs have not to pay any fee if their monthly income is up to Rs 1500. Students of such STs and SCs family get following types of scholarship for the study in colleges. This programme open a new way for hair education of tribal people.

E. Ashram School in Tribal Sub-Plan Area:

This scheme is a milestone initiative for betterment of the tribal education in India. This scheme was started in 1990-1991 with a view to provide education with residential facility to ST students.

F. Hostel Facilities for the STs Student:

This program is initiated for providing hostel accommodation facilities for STs Student who are unable to pursue their education due to their poor financial condition. The Government has established hostels for the stay of students for the purpose of study. Hostel facilities like food, cook, accommodation, light, utensils, furniture etc are provided free of cost.

G. Dress Subsidy:

Under the programmes STs and SCs students who have studying in government schools are given two sets of dresses each year. The dress also provided to STs Student free of cost.

H. Book Bank:

A book banks has been established in all educational institutions for the SCs and STs Students who has studying in medical, engineering, masters and doctoral degree. The tribal student is also benefited from the Book Bank.

I. Training and Coaching for STs Student:

The Government has established training-cum-coaching centre for the STs and SCs students to appear at UPSC and State level Service Commission examination. In every University, one such training-cum-coaching centre has been established with the assistance from the Government. The SCs, STs Students getting coaching, and training at these institutes receive a scholarship of Rs. 250/-per student per month..

J. Rajiv Gandhi National Fellowship Scheme (RGNF):

The scheme was introduced in the year 2005-2006 with the objective of providing to financial assistance the STs Students to pursue higher education such as M.Phil and Ph.D in Sciences, Humanities, Social Sciences and Engineering & Technology. University Grant Commission (UGC) took the responsibility to implement this scheme funded by Ministry of Social Justice & Empowerment and Ministry of Tribal Affairs.

K. Vocational Training Center in Tribal Areas:

Aim of the Vocational Training Center scheme is to develop the skill of STs Student depending on their qualification and present market trends. This scheme would enable them to get suitable employment or enable them to become self sufficient.

Suggestions:
Some suggestions for improvement of tribal education are as follows-

1. **Literacy Campaign:**

   Proper awareness campaign should be organized to create the awareness about the importance of education. Extensive literacy campaign in the tribal dominated districts may be undertaken on a priority basis to literate the tribal.

2. **Attitude of the Tribal parents:**

   The attitude of the tribal parents toward education should be improved through proper counseling and guidance.

3. **Relevant Study Materials in local languages:**

   All study materials should be supplied in local languages of tribes.

4. **Appointment of Local teachers and Female teachers:**

   It is suggested to appoint more tribal teachers and female teachers in the tribal areas. The ecological, cultural, psychological characteristics of tribal children should be considered carefully by the teachers in tribal areas.

5. **Stipends and Various Scholarships:**

   Since higher education among the tribes is less, special ST Scholarships should be provided to the tribal students perusing higher education, particularly in medical, engineering, and other vocational streams.

6. **Residential Schools :**

   More residential schools should be established in each states and districts and extended up to PG level in tribal areas.

7. **Social Security:**

   Social security of students, especially of adolescent girls is of great concern in residential schools.

8. Proper Monitoring:

Higher level officials should check the functioning of schools frequently relating to the teaching methods, working hours, and attendance registers. Challenging Issues of Tribal Education in India. As per my observation in this part I would to make some suggestions for improvement of tribal education in India. The important suggestions are as flow:

1. My first suggestion is the awareness campaign should be organized to create the awareness about the importance of education among the tribal parents. To more improvement of literacy campaign in the tribal dominated area to need more active role from the administrative.
2. My second suggestion is the study materials should be supplied in local languages of the tribal students. The teaching and learning process in the school should be local language.
3. Important suggestion is more residential schools should be established in each tribal dominated areas or districts. Such types of schools necessity to extend up to PG level in tribal areas for the betterment of the tribal students.
4. My another suggestion is requirement to establish separate school for girls in tribal areas with adequate classroom, teaching aids, electricity, water supply, boundary walls, play ground etc.
5. There are no sufficient higher education institutions like higher secondary schools and college in tribal areas. So government needs to establish higher secondary schools and college in the tribal areas under various governmental schemes.
6. Next Suggestion is the attitude of the tribal parents towards education is very poor it should be improved through organised more proper awareness camp, counselling and guidance.
7. It is suggested to appoint more teachers in the school of tribal areas from the tribal community. Need organised more training for the teachers to better performance towards tribal education.
8. Another suggestion is need more steps for social security of the STs Students is very important in class room and school premises, especially of adolescent girls of residential schools.
9. It is suggested to attention should be given to career or job oriented courses for the STs Student.

10. My last suggestion is proper monitoring needed for smooth functioning of the school in tribal areas by administrative authority.

Conclusion:

Education is the key to tribal development. Tribal children have very low levels of participation. Though the development of the tribes is taking place in India, but the pace of development has been rather slow. If govt. will not take some drastic steps for the development of tribal education, the status of education among tribes will be a story of distress, despair and death. Hence time has come to think it seriously about tribal education and inclusive growth. So, there is an urgent need for various govt. interventions, planners and policy makers to address this problem and allocate more funds in the central and state budgets for tribal education. Easy access and more opportunities should be provided to the tribal children in order to bring them to the mainstream of economic development.

References:

Abdulraheem, A. (2011) Education for the Economically and Socially Disadvantaged Groups in

India: An Assessment Economic Affairs Vol. 56 No. 2 June 2011 (Page 233-242)

Jha, J., Jhingran, D. (2002), Elementary Education for the Poorest and Other Deprived Groups,

Centre for Policy Research. New Delhi.

Lal, M. (2005), Education-The Inclusive Growth Strategy for the economically and socially

disadvantaged in the Society

Nair, P. (2007), "Whose Public Action? Analyzing Inter-sectoral Collaboration for Service

Delivery: Identification of Programmes for Study in India."International Development Department, Economic and Social Research Council.February.

Sedwal, M. &Sangeeta, K.(2008) Education and Social Equity with special focus on Scheduled

Castes and Scheduled Tribes in Elementary Education,NUEPA, New Delhi

Sujatha, K. (2002) Education among Scheduled Tribes. In Govinda, R. (ed.), India Education

Report: A Profile of Basic Education. New Delhi: Oxford University Press.

CHAPTER FOUR

Effect of Covid 19 on the Educational Status of Purulia

Tarak Mohan Hazari: Ph.D. Research Scholar, Department of Anthropology and Tribal Studies, Sidho Kanho Birsha University, Purulia

Samir Chandra Kuiri: Department of Chhau, Sidho Kanho Birsha University, Purulia

Dr. Savita Mishra: Principal, Vidyasagar College of Education, Phansidewa, Darjeeling, West Bengal, India

Abstract

Modern human civilization is facing a major shock around the world in the last year of the second decade of the 21st century when the advancement of modern science is at its peak. A catastrophic epidemic called Coronavirus or COVID-19 has swept across the globe, disrupting the day-to-day life of busy people, halting the pace of development. From China to Britain, Italy to America, all the most developed and powerful countries in the world are helpless today. Even in the busiest and most populous cities of the world like London, New York, there is a surprising silence today. There were announced lockdown all over India from 22nd march to prevent the corona virus. This lockdown is deeply affected on education, especially on rural area. all the educational institute are totally close. Not only closed, the schools have been developed as quarantine centres in rural area. But, As per constitution of India, education is the fundamental right of every citizen of our country. Purulia is one of the backward and deprived tribal populated district of West Bengal. According to the census of 2011, the total number of tribal population in the district is 540652, which is 18.45% of the total population of the district and 10.52% of the total ST population of West Bengal.

Introduction

Modern human civilization is facing a major shock around the world in the last year of the second decade of the 21st century when the advancement of modern science is at its peak. A catastrophic epidemic called Coronavirus or COVID-19 has swept across the globe, disrupting the day-to-day life of busy people, halting the pace of development. From China to Britain, Italy to America, all the most developed and powerful countries in the world are helpless today. Even in the busiest and most populous cities of the world like London, New York, there is a surprising silence today.

At present the statistic of the Coronavirus of the whole world is horrible. According to the World Health Organization, the number of infected people is currently around 80 lakhs, with about 4.5 lakhs dead. This graph of the number of infected and dead is constantly increasing day by day. India is not far behind in terms of victims. According to the government, the number of COVID 19 attacks in India is around 3 lakh. About 7,000 people died. The number of daily attacks is steadily rising.

The word "Corona" literally means crown. Under the electron microscope, the virus looks a lot like the crown of king. The newly discovered virus is called COVID-19 or Coronavirus Disease. The first outbreak of the disease occurred in December 2019 in China's Wuhan Province. Although the virus infects people of all ages, those who have low immunity and those who are older people are more likely to be severely infected. According to doctors, the symptoms of this disease are mainly fever, dry cough, fatigue. It can also cause colds, shortness of breath, sore throat, and even diarrhoea.

Originally this Coronavirus was coming at the very last moment of 2019. The first attack of Coronavirus happened in December 2019. The symptoms of the disease first appear on the body of a butcher in the Wuhan province of China, when the world celebrates the end of the Year's festivities and waits for the New Year. The disease gradually spread to other vendors in the meat market. The number of patients is increasing day by day. And then the deaths are also increasing. Then start the activeness for research. According to various doctors, the initial symptoms of this disease are mild fever, cold, cough, and shortness of breath, which eventually leads to death in many people. It gradually spread beyond the Chinese city of Wuhan to other cities. The virus also spreads to peoples of other countries living in China. And later, the germs of Coronavirus are carried to their country through them. After China, its influence is gradually increasing in European countries. Italy was the first attacked country after China. The healthcare system of Italy is one of the most modern in the world, but for the attack of Corona virus that high-quality health care is practically crippled. Day by day, COVID-19 has gradually spread to other countries like Spain, France, Netherlands, United States, South Korea, etc. and this way the world is gradually attacked.

About the Tribes

The tribes are the aborigional community of india . according to 2011 censuss, there are live 10.2 crore tribal people in this country who are also known as Adivasi and the constitution of India has designated "tribes" as Scheduled Tribes (Art 366).At the present time around 697 tribes recogniged as central government and around 75 recognized as Particularly Vulnerable Tribal Groups (PVTG) according to Article 342.There are 40 Scheduled Tribe communities and 3 PVTG found in WB according to the census report of 2011.

Purulia is one of the backward and deprived tribal populated district of West Bengal. According to the censuss of 2011, the total number of tribal population in the district is 540652, which is 18.45% of the total population of the district and 10.52% of the total ST population of West Bengal. Among these population, the major five communities are Santal(60%), Bhumij(18%), Sabar(7%), Munda(6%) and Bihor(1%).

Study area and People

This study is carried out in two blocks of the south western part of Purulia district, Baghmundi and Balarampur. In the Baghmundi and Balarampur areas, the Ajodhya Hills form the main highlands, forming the drainage divide between the basins of the Subrnarekha and the Kangsabati. The elevation ranges from 475 to 700 m. The Balarampur CD block is bounded by the Arsha CD block on the north, the Barabazar CD block on the east and on the south, the Nimdih CD block in the Seraikela Kharsawan district of Jharkhand and the Baghmundi CD block on the west.

The Balarampur CD block has an area of 300.88 km2. It has 1 panchayat samity, 7 gram panchayats, 92 gram sansads (village councils), 90 mouzas, 89 inhabited villages and 1 census town. Balarampur police station serves this block. Headquarters of this CD block is at Baghadih. Gram panchayats of the Balarampur block/panchayat samiti are: Balarampur, Bara-Urma, Bela, Darda, Genrua, Ghatbera-Kerowa and Tentlo. According to the 2011 Census of India the Balarampur CD block had a total population of 137,950, of which 113,519 were rural and 24,431 were urban. There were 70,995 (51%) males and 66,955 (49%) females. There were 20,118 persons in the age range of 0 to 6 years. The Scheduled Castes numbered 16,427 (11.91%) and the Scheduled Tribes numbered 43,738 (31.71%). Census Towns in the Balarampur CD block are Balarampur (24,431). Large villages (with 4,000+ population) in the Balarampur CD block are (2011 census figures in brackets): Genrua (6,454). Some others villages in the Balarampur CD block are Bela (3,436), Darda (2,619), Tentlo (2,924), Ghatbera (1,858) and Keraya (2,140).

According to the 2011 census, the total number of literate persons in the Balarampur CD block was 71,176 (60.40% of the population over 6 years) out of which males numbered 44,950 (74.18% of the male population over 6 years) and females numbered 26,226 (45.82%) of the female population over 6 years). The gender disparity (the difference between female and male literacy rates) was 28.35%.

Baghmundi is located at 23°12′N 86°03′E. The Subarnarekha forms the interstate boundary between West Bengal and Jharkhand in the Jhalda I CD block and a small portion of Bahgmundi CD block. The Bagmundi-Bandwan uplands is an area that has descended from the Ranchi Plateau. In the Baghmundi and Balarampur areas, the Ajodhya Hills form the main highlands, forming the drainage divide between the basins of the Subrnarekha and the Kangsabati. The elevation ranges from 475 to 700 m.

Baghmundi CD block is bounded by Jhalda II and Arsha CD blocks on the north, the Balarampur CD block on the east, the Kukru CD block, in the Seraikela Kharsawan district of Jharkhand, on the south, and the Jhalda I CD block on the west.

The Baghmundi CD block has an area of 427.95 km2. It has 1 panchayat samity, 8 gram panchayats, 92 gram sansads (village councils), 142 mouzas and 138 inhabited villages. Baghmundi police station serves this block. Headquarters of this CD block is at Patardi. Gram panchayats of the Baghmundi CD block/panchayat samiti are: Ajodhya, Baghmundi, Birgram, Burda-Kalimati, Matha, Serengdih, Sindri and Tunturi-Suisa. According to the 2011 Census of India, the Baghmundi CD block had a total population of 135,579, all of which were rural. There were 69,520 (51%) males and 66,059 (49%) females. There were 21,992 persons in the age range of 0 to 6 years. The Scheduled Castes numbered 14,042 (10.36%) and the Scheduled Tribes numbered 34,038 (25.11%). Large villages (with 4,000+ population) in the Baghmundi CD block are Baghmundi (4,039), Burda (5,159) and Sindri (4,138). Other villages in the Baghmundi CD block are (2011 census figures in brackets): Ajodhya (1,468), Patardi (1,609), Birgram (3,722), Kalimati

(1,961), Serengdi (305), Tunturi (2,037), Suisa (2,649) and Matha (624).

According to the 2011 census, the total number of literate persons in the Baghmundi CD block was 64,939 (57.17% of the population over 6 years) out of which males numbered 42,019 (72.14% of the male population over 6 years) and females numbered 22,920 (41.42%) of the female population over 6 years). The gender disparity (the difference between female and male literacy rates) was 30.72%.

Impact of COVID 19 on socio economic life Purulia

As a result of the lockdown, public are suffering a lot. All those peoples are most affected who were at their relative's house on that day, some in the hospital, some on a trip, some on their way home from workplace, and some were out of the house for other work. For this condition there are created an extreme stalemate. Many people are facing on financial crisis or food crisis. Not only getting stuck, the families who lives depended on their daily income were most affected by this lockdown across the country to prevent the Coronavirus. As a result of the closing of the market, their daily income was completely cut off. At that time, due to the closure of the market, a huge amount of vegetables and other agricultural crops were destroyed every day. The farmer's hand fell on his head. Every day, litters of milk and dairy products were wasted. Due to the complete lockdown of the transport system, a lot of trucks got stuck in different places, which caused a lot of damage the perishable goods in the cargo trucks. These losses are undoubtedly enough to add fuel in the fire of India's crisis.Anticipating the news of crisis of the lockdown, many people started stored up various necessities and food items, also those who did not have sufficient money, they also started buying household items from their savings.As a result, gradually the lack of money came to their door.The government promised to provide various rations for free as soon as the lockdown was announced, but there was no guarantee that it would reach to those needy people in how many days.On the other hand at the same time, some dishonest traders create artificial crises and increase the prices of various commodities. And as a result of all these, the people are facing an extreme misery.

Daily laborers of different strata of the society, i.e. those who depended on their daily income, such as rickshaw or auto drivers, various hawkers, house builder, labour of brick kilns and other unorganized workers, various small shopkeepers of footpath, etc., stop earning completely. In this situation their daily life is drowned into extreme darkness. They become disoriented even though they are not infected with the deadly disease like

Coronavirus.

This is not the end of everything, then comes the "migrant labour problem", one of the biggest problems in the country at present. While other problems have to be faced during this difficult time of the Corona epidemic, but no other country in the world has faced this "migrant labor problem". And this is the difference between India and other countries. Many people from different states come to work in different industrial areas or industrial cities of the country. But when everything is closed due to the lockdown, the owner of these industries or work place refuses to keep them and also refuses take responsibility for fear of losses and virus infection. As a result, these people, who work for daily wages, face a deep crisis of living and eating. Somewhere they were forcibly evicted and without food they were anxious to return home, but at this time of lockdown all vehicles were almost closed and security was very tight all around, so the only recourse for them to return home was on foot.But they did not have the minimum food which is required to cover the distance of 200-300 km or more across one or more states to reach their home, and in many places police beatings were not excluded. As a result, many migrant workers fell ill and many died.

As a result, the government loosened the rush and launched "workers‘ special" train to take them home. Various state governments arrange buses for their return. Many are ready to return home on their own initiative. In this case also many accidents happen due to negligence. Last but not least, many people are infected with the corona virus because they come from different infected areas in several big cities, and as a result, the Coronavirus spreads from the city to the rural area of India. It also makes rural life unbearable with terror. Also, Purulia was no exception.

As easy as it is to keep people in "quarantine" in urban areas, it is not possible in rural areas, and almost all area of these two blocks are rural. like the town, there is no separate management for everyone in the village, not everyone has a separate room for the family, so "home quarantine" is virtually impossible in the villages. Relying on drinking water is basically tube well, everyone consumes water from the same tube well. The same pond is used for bathing. In that pond, utensils are washed, also clothes are washed. Although rivers are used for these purposes in the riverside villages, many villages still drink the water of that river. As a result, if one person is infected, the chances of infection among the rest of the villagers are very high. And rural health care is not as good as in the city. Another notable issue is the lack of awareness, which is one of the biggest problems in rural areas. At the same time, many people in the village still consider its a luxury to follow the hygiene measures like to use a mask for going outside or to wash their hands frequently with hand sanitizer to protect from the COVID-19. At the same time, superstitions and bigotry are major obstacles to the development of rural health, and now there are adding a new dimension called "rumours". Thus,it can say by see the overall, that no villages is safe from the infection of the corona.

Present status of education in Purulia

Purulia is one of the westernmost districts of West Bengal. It is an important parts of "Jangolmohol" and also Chotanagpur plateau. There are total 3292 ICDS centre in Purulia district which carry the pre schooling system, from this the number of benefit children are 104442. There are total 2971 primary schools are present. The total number of secondary and higher secondary school are 328.

There was established a university at 2010 namely Sidho-Kanho-Birsha university. After the establishment of this university the scenario of higher education of the district are slowly grade up. There are 21 affiliated degree collage and 1 professional college under the university. 4 polytechnic college are situated in Purulia district. Besides, near the university there are located "Sainik School". One of the biggest and important Sainik School of all over India. It is a bright star of the educational map of Purulia. According to the cencuss 2011, total literacy rate of the district is 65.38%.

Reasons for the Educational Backwardness among ST community in th:

The main reasons and factors that responsible for such backwardness in education among tribal communities are high dropout rate, low enrolment, poverty, low attention to education, lack of motivation, lack of proper guidance in education, low income and school infrastructure etc.

1. Tribal education is greatly affected due to child marriage, poor academic performance, lack of awareness, poor understanding level, lack of motivation, low ambition etc. Also, the level of awareness among tribals is somewhat lower than that of non-tribals due to low ambition. Which greatly affects their later life.

2. Various family factors are also responsible for their backwardness. Their family's poverty, unemployment, parents' level of education, low income and sometimes even family conflicts due to alcoholism cause huge disruption in their educational life.Duc to the poor economic condition

of the family, children are forced to engage in child labor for money. And all these factors hinder them greatly in higher education.

3. Also various environmental factors surrounding them, such as distance from their home to school, poor school infrastructure, shortage of teachers, lack of girls' school and hostel facilities etc. also affect their educational life.

Effect of Covid-19 on education of Purulia

There were announced lockdown all over India from 22nd march to prevent the corona virus. This lockdown is deeply affected on education, especially on rural area. all the educational institute are totally close. Not only closed, the schools have been developed as quarantine centres in rural area. According to a report of UNESCO, that the coronavirus pandemic will adversely impact over 290 million students across 22 countries. The UNESCO estimates that about 32 crores students are affected in India, including those in schools and colleges. And naturally the results are bound to fall in Purulia.

There are one of the alternative ways to continue the educational system is e-learning or digital learning during this pandemic situation. Day by dayit's become popular all over the country. This e-learning is done through various methods, like video conference, group chat, group calling, recorded voice or video or power point presentation etc. As a result of getting these facilities at home, time and labour both will be saved.

But, all of this modern technologyis unavailable in the backword rural area of Baghmundi and Balarampur block. There are several obstacles for this e- learning facilities. Not all the people in the village have the equipment they need for this e-learning. And for online studies, the most important things are the internet. And although this internet service of village area is better than before, but its price is so high that it seems like a luxury to the recent unemployed peoples. So, the students in those families are reluctant to use this online education system. As a result, on this era of competition, they are falling behind the urban student's day by day.

There are two collage in these two blocks namely Balarampur Collage at Balarampur and Netaji Subhas Ashram Mahabidyalay at Baghmundi. In this lockdown period, several departments of these collage carry their classes through online and social media. Incidentally, while online classes are somewhat possible in higher education, but this online classes or e-learningare absolutely unrealistic in primary and secondary level schools.

Because there is no any infrastructure in those backward area of Baghmundi and Balarampur block. There are total 182 primary, secondary and higher secondary school inBalarampur block and 214 in Baghmundi block. All about the students are totally deprived from the digital learning for the absence of infrastructure. And its deeply affected on their educational life. Because of the long-term financial crisis, many will be forced to drop out of school, and looking for various work to help their family. The condition of the girls is more dire. Because many are being forced to get married to reduce the economic problem of the family.

Although the online system could be implemented in colleges, not everyone could use it equally. As a result, many have avoided it and many have been forced to avoid.Another notable issue is tuition,Nowadays, in addition to school and college, tuition has a special significance in student life. However, students from financially indigent families in the village depend on school and college education throughout the year.Meanwhile, although the school and college are closed indefinitely, the tuitions have started after a temporary break. As a result, some students are falling behind. AndThese deprivations created a mental inequalityamong the students. And these are of the major effect of COVID-19 pandemic on education.

Conclusion

As human civilization has progressed, nature has lost its natural features and the environment has lost its balance. As a result, on the one hand, natural disasters are increasing, same as the tendency of diseases are increasing in human society. The Corona epidemic is no exception, which is one of the scares of thetoday's modern world.But like the other five common infectious diseases, it is also a contagious disease, but the novel corona virus poses a major question to human civilization around the world.The man who declares himself a world champion today is always; this novel corona virus has stopped the progress of the proud civilization of that man in an instant.As a result, the two pillars of human civilization, the economy and the education sector have suffered the most.

But after the darkness there is present a flash of light. No one can deny that there is something good in the midst of so much evil. That is what happened to the corona virus. Putting all the bad news aside, the habit of washing hands repeatedly to prevent corona will undoubtedly benefit people.Most notably, the long-running lockdown has reduced the level of environmental pollution in almost all countries. As a result, the environment has become a little fresher, the weather has become clearer. Yet people are terrified, because on the one hand, unemployment, the financial crisis of poorpeople's, the collapsed economy and on the other hand, rapidly spread of various rumours with the spread of the virus. At the same time, the impact of the corona virus on the education sector is undoubtedly a great loss. As a result, not only the students but also it affected their guardian. In this case, the most affected is the rural society. However, it is not known that, how long it will take to get back to normal life after overcoming all the effects. It remains to be seen what the government will do.

Reference:

Ordóñez de Pablos, P. (2015) Impact of Economic Crisis on Education and the Next-Generation Workforce, IGI Global, 9781466694552

Patra, Uttam & Gayak, Jibanbandhu & Karim, Sk & Halder, Sourav & Sen, Arup & Paul, Gobindo. (2021). a comparative study of tribal education development in India: with special references to Purulia district, West Bengal. Journal of Critical Reviews. 8. 110-121. 10.31838/jcr.08.01.1.

Agarwal, H. Pandey, G.N. (2013)Impact of E-learning on education,International Journal of Science and Research, 12(2), 146-148

https://bigyan.org.in/2020/03/20/corona-virus-facts/

https://covidindia.org/

https://www.mohfw.gov.in/

Shrivastav, C. (2012) e-Learning, Challenges and Impact on Education: Contextual Factor and Development, Intelectual Learning, *Technology and Ideal Learning Systems, LAP LAMBERT Academic Publishing.*

https://en.wikipedia.org/wiki/ Baghmundi_(community_development_block)

http://www.purulia.gov.in/distAdmin/departments/health/ rural_health.html

http://purulia.nic.in/services/notice/general/COVID_6.pdf

CHAPTER FIVE

Indigenous Peoples: Tradition, Language and Literature

Usharani Mahato: Ph.D Research Scholar, Department of Anthropology and Tribal Studies, Sidho – Kanho - Birsha University, Purulia

Dr. Sudip Bhui: Assistant Professor, Department of Anthropology and Tribal Studies, Sidho – Kanho -Birsha University, Purulia

Abstract

Indigenous peoples today the most disadvantaged and vulnerable groups of people in the world.Observing the dynamics of history, it is clear that the daily life of these indigenous peoples is driven by hard struggle, tolerance, and bitterness. The great heritage, culture, knowledge, language, and symbols of the people are being lost.The Santals are an ethnic group in India, the third largest in terms of the indigenous population. They have a strong connection with tradition.The house of santals is usually made from clay or mud. Beautiful designs are painted on the walls. Santali is the most widely spoken language among Austro- Asiatic speakers in India. The Santali language is a part of the Austroasiatic family.By worshiping the nature of the Sarna religion, the santals gained a new sense of values and ethics, the concept of equality. To understand the life and world view of the indigenous people we need to be more involved in their imaginary world.

Introduction

The United Nations affirms that Indigenous Peoples are inheritors and practitioners of unique cultures and ways of relating to people and the environment. It recognized that Indigenous Peoples have retained social, cultural, economic, and political characteristics that are distinct from those of the dominant societies in which they live. Indigenous Peoples from around the world share common problems related to the protection of their rights as distinct peoples, while also retaining cultural differences.

Indigenous peoples are culturally distinct societies and communities. The term "indigenous" has prevailed as a generic term for many years. In some countries, there may be a preference for other terms including tribes, first peoples/nations, aboriginals, ethnic groups, Adivasi, and janajati.

The Declaration establishes a universal framework of minimum standards for the survival, dignity, well-being, and rights of the world's indigenous peoples. The Declaration addresses both individual and collective rights; cultural rights and identity; rights to education, health, employment, language, and others. It outlaws discrimination against indigenous peoples and promotes their full and effective participation in all matters that concern them. It also ensures their right to remain distinct and to pursue their priorities in economic, social, and cultural development.

In the pre-colonial period, we can call all the people who have traditionally lived in certain lands, with distinct languages, cultures, social customs, and nature friendly. More than 37 crore people carry this tradition in more than 70 countries all over the world. Compared to world history, the traditional trend of indigenous people in our country is obvious.

Observing the dynamics of history, it is clear that the daily life of these indigenous peoples is driven by hard struggle, tolerance, and bitterness. The great heritage, culture, knowledge, language, and symbols of the people are being lost. NASA - The Sixteenth Shuttle Marie Golda Ross, a world-renowned female mathematician, and engineer from the Cherokee Native American community played a key role in NASA's action plan for rocket science, the US Military Reserve. John Harrington of the Chikas Indigenous Peoples of America participated in the Mission, in 2002 and went into space. Susan Picotti of the Omaha Indigenous Group of America opens the first hospital in the region as the first doctor. Even Angelina Jolie, one of Hollywood's highest-earning actresses and one of the three Golden Globe Award-winning actresses, is descended from Aboriginal people.

The Santals are an ethnic group in eastern India, the third largest in terms of the indigenous population (after Bhil and Gond). Santals are the largest ethnic group in the Indian state of Jharkhand and are also present in the states of Assam, Tripura, Bihar, Odisha, and West Bengal. The Santals believe that they originated from the seven pairs of children of the 'AdiManav' and the 'Manavi' PilchuBuro (Haram) and PilchuBuri. That is why the Santals are divided into seven tribes. First, there were seven gotras and later five more gotras emerged among them making a total of twelve gotras. Totem belief is prevalent among the Santals. Each tribe is known by the name of their ancestors or plants, animals and birds, etc. The people of the Hansda tribe believe that they originated from ducks. So the Santals of Hansdagotra are forbidden to eat duck.

Review of literature

It is estimated that there are more than 370 million indigenous people spread across 70 countries worldwide. Practicing unique traditions, they retain social, cultural, economic, and political characteristics that are distinct from those of the dominant societies in which they live. For generations, Indigenous peoples have sought recognition of their identities, way of life, and their right to traditional lands, territories, and natural resources. Throughout history, however, their rights have been and continue to be violated. Indigenous peoples today, are arguably among the most disadvantaged and vulnerable groups of people in the world. The international community now recognizes that special measures are required to protect their rights and maintain their distinct cultures and way of life.The tribes of the northeast have a high level of politicisation, literacy and a high standard of living compared to their counterparts in other parts. The tribes were alienated from their own lands. The landlords and moneylenders of the plains gradually replaced the tribal landowners. The survey done by B. K. Roy Burman (1972) shows that the tribals are the most backward as because of their low literacy and primitive economy. The dominant thinking today is in favour of assimilation of the tribal people into the national mainstream without any disruption. It is not easy to have both dissolution and assimilation at the same time (Roy, 1970).

As a follower of the geniuses of the Indus Valley Civilization, in the Rigveda, in the Ramayana and the Mahabharata in 1600 BC, in the Arthashastra of Kautilya in 320 BC, according to the thirteenth inscription of MahamatiAshoka, they played an ancient history in India and South Asia.

In the middle Ages, the good governance of the Munda, Asura, Nag, and Veel dynasties in central and northern India has been marked by glorious trends. The Malpahariya, Chuar, and Pike Rebellions, Kol Rebellion, Santal Rebellion, and Munda Rebellion played pivotal roles in the successive movements of the freedom struggle. The world map shows the history of the great struggles of Indigenous peoples in the United States, Canada, Mexico, Brazil, etc. in the Amazon region.

According to the 2011 census, the total tribal population of India stands at 8.6 percent in 27 out of 29 states and 3 out of 7 union territories.

Paul Olaf Bodding, a Norwegian is one of the famous missionaries who are well-known by the santal tribe. He studied their culture and traditions and learned their language as well. He completed the translation of the santal Bible in 1914.

Methodology

For this qualitative study, I used interviews and group discussions with indigenous people especially the Santal tribe and other villagers. Depth interviews are the chief method for data collection in this study. Focus group discussion was also an important method. Secondary data were collected from references. I have taken the help of various articles and books to know about the literature, language, and culture of indigenous people, especially the Santal tribes.

Culture

There are twelve clans among the Santals, they are Hansda, Murmu, Kisku, Hembrom, Mandi, Soren, Tudu, Baskey, Besra, Chore, Pauria, and Bedea. The last two clans are no longer distinct. They cannot marry a member of the same clan. Primarily forest and agricultural, these people carry along a rich cultural heritage. That culture is expressed through their dances, song, and rituals. They are also actively involved in animal husbandry. They are one of the most primitive castes among the oldest tribal groups in India. The santal village is surrounded by agricultural fields, pastures, ponds, and a common place of worship known as Jaher Than. Located at the village outsides the jaher than is the sacred groove comprising of Sal trees within which their deities are believed to be residing. Usually, the santal villages are large. But sometimes we saw small villages. Their houses enclosed within boundaries are arranged in a linear pattern on both sides of a wide village street.

Every santal village is headed by a headman called Majhi. He is assisted by his assistant called jog majhi. Every village has a priest called naike, who carries out religious activities in the village. The largest house in the village belongs to Majhi. He is the secular headman of the village. In front of his house, Majhi-than is located. It is the seat of the spirit of the founder headman of the village.

The house of santals is usually made from clay or mud. Beautiful designs are painted on the walls. Structures of animals, birds, or other familiar figures are made on the walls. The santals have a strong connection with tradition.

Santal houses are large, neat, and clean as well as attractive with multi-colored paintings on the outside walls. Each house has a long verandah. Wall paintings are usually done by tribal women and girls of the village. The content and elements of the wall painting collect themselves. They take time out of their routine household work. Wall painting is prevalent in most areas of Purulia district. Santal, Bhumij, Kora, Mahali, Munda, Kharia, etc. tribal communities live in Purulia district, but santals paint the most wall paintings. The kurmis of purulia painted this wall painting. Wall paintings in mud houses are temporary. These wall paintings are usually painted before BandnaParab in the month of Kartik. All the tribal community makes these wall paintings specific to the new moon in the month of kartik. All houses are repaired. Starting from the entrance of the house to the yard, gohal, residence everywhere is decorated with alpana.

The wall paintings of the santals community usually extend up to a height of five to six feet from the ground. Santali wall paintings are mainly composed of geometric shapes and color combinations. Mahato, kora, bhumij, etc. communities usually have pictures of lotus flowers on their walls. The petals of this lotus are filled with various colors. Sometimes the flowering plant is seen emerging from a tub or urn, spreading branches on both sides and blooming on the branches. This lotus is said to be the symbol of Manbhum's wall paintings (*MatirGhorerDewalChitra,* TapanKar*).* Very smooth walls are coated with relatively light-colored silt. The color of this soil is white. While this clay coating is still wet, the picture is drawn by drawing marks on it with the tips of the fingers.

Tradition

The santals have a strong connection with tradition. The feet of guests are usually washed with water before they are to enter the house. They greet relatives in a very peculiar way. Elder people usually, stretch out their hands and place them above the heads of the younger ones. Elder women usually, bring their palms together facing upwards and lift them towards their forehead as a sign of accepting the greeting. In-laws have a different way of greeting each other which is called Johar (Saren, P. and Jamir, W. 2021). These are not found in any other community. These make them maintain peace among themselves. These salutations increase their bond of brotherhood.

The santals have their instruments. They are used during weddings, festivals, and other occasions. Weddings are conducted with great excitement and music.

Dance is one of the important parts of their weddings and festivals. After the wedding, the bride washes the feet of her husband's brothers and sister. This is the last time she touches her husband's elder brother physically. During the washing of feet, the bride washes the feet of her husband first. A married woman does not leave her hair in public places. She is also not supposed to sit on a bed.

When a child is born, the santal midwife cuts the umbilical cord of the child. After five days, the midwife calls all the village members for a meal at the birthplace. She also gives oil to everyone who comes as a sign of welcome. During these five days, the mother is not allowed to touch any household items. After this event, she is suitable to perform household chores or touch household items.

Language

An important feature of Indian civilization is its huge linguistic diversity. Our pronunciation differs according to the type of geographical region. After independence, the states of India were reorganized based on language. Only those languages that had alphabets were considered, those that had no traditional alphabet and therefore no printed literature get their kingdoms. Schools and colleges were created only for government-recognized languages. Although the non-alphabetic languages were rich in wisdom accumulated in their oral traditions, they were not fortunate enough to have educational institutions. It is in the context of this extreme neglect that the creativity of India's original languages has to be understood. The history of tribal in the last 70 years is a history of forced evictions, alienation from land rights, increasing materialization violence, and the narrative of state violence in response. In any measure of development, tribal always scores lowest. The condition of nomadic peoples is even worse. It is amazing that despite fighting against so many adversities, the tribes have managed to preserve their language and contribute to the wonderful diversity of languages in India.

One of the defining characteristics of tribals is their linguistic heritage. Adivasis are generally characterized as 'shyness', living in remote places and groups are clinging to their language. People speaking Santali are called santals. Santali language to start with, never had any script of its own.

Santali is the most widely spoken language among Austro- Asiatic speakers in India and is also one of the officially recognized minority languages. The Santali language is a part of the Austroasiatic family. Their language belongs to the Munda, Ho, Mahli, Bhumij, and Kharia family of language. Santals did not have a written language until the nineteenth century. The script is developed by PanditRaghunathMurmu in 1925. Alchiki has 30 alphabets and is written from left to right. The script is made up of 6 vowels and 24 consonants.

Scandinavian Christian saints who came to SantalParganas in 1867 learned the santal language to translate their scriptures. For the sake of their work, the missionaries initiated the Santali collaborators in the Roman script; those collaborators collected stories from different places and gave them. The aim of Christian saints was the radical reformation of santals. They wanted to do this by gradually tying the world of faith of the santals to the category of folklore so that they gradually leave the worship of their idols and take refuge in Christ. In 1890 P. O. Boding came to SantalParganas and took this work forward and after 35 years the Santali Dictionary was published in five volumes (Carrin, 2019).

In santali literary expression, the insertion of different people's memories is seen. These memory narratives are mainly based on the two axes of actual historical events and rural stories. These memories refer to two types of periods; one is the pre-santal revolt which reflects the pain of their deprivation and all loss: two, the post-santal revolt which reflects the sorrow and despair of the then impoverished, famine-stricken, and exploited santal people. After coming under direct colonial rule, the santal community was forced to pay land taxes and thus increasingly became part of a monetary system.

Santali literature after 1890 bears witness to the cultural and social changes seen by their authors. Most of the evidence of the changes in Santali social life as a result of the British colonial rule has remained in the rulers' documents. Judging from the perspective of that reality, Santali writer's narratives are very important. Their main aim was to inform mission associates about the Santali language and culture as well as to preserve information about their society. They wanted to convince the missionaries that they had their religion by professing their own religious beliefs and trusting in gods. They wanted to present their society to the British rulers and European missionaries by talking about their knowledge and judicial system. (Carrin 2021).

Among the missionaries' collections were Santali myths about their gods, clans, and village life. Also from Santali narratives, one can learn about various aspects of santal social life such as kinship, marriage, social etiquette, customs, and bonds. (Anderson, Carrin, Soren, 2011).In 2004,

Santali was included in the 8th schedule of the Indian constitution as a scheduled language.

Literature

The emergence of the Santali language through script created boundaries in a practical sense. (Choksi, 2013) Santali literature can be broadly divided into three major periods. The first stage was Santali literature written in Bengali script under the leadership of missionaries from 1880 onwards. The second phase began in the 1930s when RaghunathMurmu tried to convey social messages through the creation of mythological narratives. The main objective of his campaign was the spread of education; he firmly believed that poverty could be eradicated through the spread of education. In the third phase, Santali literature was able to exert a very important influence. The literature of this period deals with the condition of the workers, their deprivations, protests, and even occasional calls for armed resistance. (Carrin 2019).

In the 1930s RaghunathMurmu strongly opposed the Santali literature written in various Indian scripts and created a new alphabet known as 'Alchiki'. (Carrin 2021). The introduction of Alchiki in the 1950s was able to give the youth a sense of identity. In 1964, RaghunathMurmu and other experts formed an organization called ASECA (Adivasi – Socio-Educational and Cultural Association). The main objective of this organization was the preservation of the Santali language and culture. The All India Santal Council and Later the All India santal writers Association worked for the promotion of Alchiki. By worshiping the nature of the Sarna religion, the santals gained a new sense of values and ethics, the concept of equality. It helps them to develop resistance against social classification and racism. Later the youth community started writings drama on social issues. In 1936 the collection of seventeen Santali poems first, *OnorheBahaDalwa* (Branch of Flower) was composed by Paul JujherSoren (Tudu, 2013). Thus poetry was the first foreign literary genre that was adopted by the Santali writers. The genre of drama was introduced in Santali literature by PanditRaghunathMurmu'sBiduChandan and KherwalBir in 1942 and 1946 respectively (Mahapatra, 1971).

The genre of novels, in Santali literature, entered through translation. R.R. kisku first translated R. Carstairs's historical novel Harman's Village (1935) into Santali as HarmavaAtu in 1946 (Hembrom, 2010). The new generation of writers portrayed village life, problems in ruining areas, and various school events through their writings. Writers of Santali language take initiative on various local issues. In addition to alleviating the suffering of the local villagers, they want to gain some kind of legal and political power by emphasizing their tribal identity. (Xaxa 2000). The constant political struggle against poverty is reflected in Santali literature.

Development Policy of Indigenous People

For the first time since its independence, the government of India is proposing the formulation of a National Policy on Scheduled Tribes. The policy seeks to bring Scheduled Tribes into the mainstream of society through a multipronged approach to their all-around development without disturbing their distinct culture. Scheduled Tribes are those, which are notified as such by the president of India under Article 342 of the Constitution.

Until the 1950s the Elwin remained only among the tribal peoples of central India. After independence, he was sent to North East India. In 1953, the government of India decided to open a special branch for the North East Indian Civil Service. Elwin is asked to help the government by choosing officers for this new branch. Elwin established identity was that of an anthropologist, scholar, author, and indigenous favorite. Towards the end of his life, he became known as an administrator and policymaker for tribal development. In 1959, the govt. of India asked Elwin to prepare a report on tribal development. He said if any plan for the development of the tribe is to be successful, it must have the touch of the tribal mentality: 'if possible, we must see through the eyes of the tribal and from the point of view of the tribal. Respect for tribal life practices and tribal culture was the strong foundation of his proposed tribal policy.

Jawaharlal Nehru in the preface to Elwin's A Philosophy for NEFA (North Eastern Frontier Agency) wrote about the key features of Elwin's proposed tribal development: the problems of tribal areas cannot be allowed to disappear or we show no interest in them. In today's world that is not possible and it is not desirable. At the same time, excessive patrolling of these areas and especially the sending of large numbers of outsiders should be avoided. We must work between these two extreme positions. Various aspects of development can be considered such as communication systems, medicine, education, and improved farming methods. However, development activities must be carried out within the broad framework of these five basic principles:

First, communities will essentially evolve along their path of excellence and we will refrain from imposing anything. We will encourage their traditional arts and cultural activities.

Secondly, we should inform them of their right to land and forest.

Thirdly, we should train and create a team from among the tribal themselves to do the administration and development work. Initially, some technical experts from outside will no doubt be needed. But we should not employ too many outsiders in tribal areas.

Fourth, we should not over-inform these regions or overwhelm them with multiple projects.

Fifth, the evaluation of the results should not be based only on statistics or the amount of money spent. It has to do, with the quality of human character that emerges through the process.

The national policy aims at addressing each of these problems in a concrete way.

Conclusion

Indigenous Peoples today, are arguably among the most vulnerable groups of people in the world. The international community, including the United Nations, now recognizes that special measures are required to protect their rights and maintain their distinct cultures and way of life. Indigenous people are so diverse in terms of ethnic, cultural, and linguistic characteristics that they cannot be identified as a general category of mankind. With the development of Santali literature, its relation developed with various cultural and political trends.

Indigenous, tribes or Adivasis or natives- whatever we call them, non-Natives are still not fully understood in scholarly practice. Their lives and our knowledge are still contradictory. To understand the life and world view of the indigenous people we need to be more involved in their imaginary world. For this reason, the importance of language and literature cannot be ignored in understanding the condition of the indigenous people of India. Unfortunately, when these people are trying to express their ideas and imaginations in literature, the only medium of expression is their language, which is facing a terrible challenge and is in danger of almost disappearing. Santali writers prepared themselves in such a way that they could influence the people of their community. They prepared their communal positions based on the events of daily life. Many Santali stories revolve around the lives of revolutionaries.

Reference

Anderson, Peter B., Marine Carrin and Santosh Kumar Soren (2011), from Fire Rain to Rebellion: Reasserting Ethnic Identity through Narrative,

New Delhi: Manohar.

Bodding, P.O., A santal dictionary (5 vols), Det Norske VidenskspsAkademi. (Oslo 1932-36)

BosuMullick, Samar (1991), "The concept of Supreme Being" in BosuMullick, Samar (ed). Cultural Chotanagpur: Unity in Diversity, New Delhi: Uppal Publisher.

Carrin, M. and H. Tambs-Lyche (2008), An Encounter of Peripheries: Santals Missionaries and their Changing Worlds, 1867-1900, Delhi: Manohar.

Carrin, M., (2019) 'The making of an encyclopedic dictionary: How P. O. Bodding Re- enchanted santal words', *Journal of Adivasis and Indigenous studies*, pp, 1-13.

Carrin, M., (2021) 'Santal Rationality as empowerment', P. B. Andersen, R. Mehdi and A. Prakash (eds) Re- interrogating Civil Society in South Asia, Critical Perspectives from India, Pakistan and Bangladesh, London: Routled, pp. 249-272.

Choksi, N. (2014) 'Scripting the border: script practices and territorial imagination among Santali speakers in eastern India', *International Journal of the Sociology of Language*, Vol.5,No.1 ,pp. 47-63.

Chottopadhyaya, Debiprasad., (1959) Lokayata: A study in Ancient Indian Materialism, Bombay: peoples publishing House.

Elwin, Verrier (2016[1957]), A Philosophy for NEFA, Delhi: Isha Books.

Hembrom, P. (2010). Santali SahityerItihaas. Kolkata :Nirmal Book Agency.

Mahapatra, J. (1971). The patterns of Dust. Bhubneshwar: BooklandIntermation.

Munda, Ram Dayal (1989), 'The Bases of Cultural Identity of Chotanagpur', Religion and Society, 36 (2).

Rana. K., and M. Sarkar, with S Das and M Gain (2020), Living World of Adivasis of West Bengal- An Ethnographic Exploration, Kolkata: The Asiatic Society and Pratichi Institute.

Rana, S., (2019), 'Santalhulerdersobachhar', Prabandhasangrha, Kolkata :Gangchil.

Roy Burman, B.K. (1972): Tribal Demography: A preliminary Survey, in K.S. Singh (ed.), Tribal Situation in India, Indian Institute of Advanced Study, Simla

Roy, Sarat Chandra (1912), TheMundas and their Country, Calcutta: City Book Society.

Roy, Sarat Chandra and Ramesh Chandra Roy, (1937), TheKharias, vol. II. Ranchi: Man in India.

. Roy, S.C. (1970): The Mundas and their Country (reprint), Asia Publishing House, Bombay, pp. 34-40

Soren, P. and Jamir, W. (2021), The Santals: Their Culture and Traditions, In book: Trends in sociology, psychology and anthropology, volume-2 (pp. 79-97) Edition: 1 chapter: 5 Publisher: AkiNik Publications

Tudu, K. C. (2013). Santali sahityakaudbhavaurvikas. Ranchi: Santali sahityaparisad.

Xaxa, V., (1999) 'Tribes as Indigenous People of India' EPW, vol. 34, (51), pp 3589-3595.

https://www.un.org/development/desa/indigenouspeoples/about-us.html

https://www.un.org/development/desa/indigenouspeoples/international-day-of-the-worlds-indigenous-peoples.html

https://www.un.org/en/development/desa/news/social/suffering-of-indigenous.html

Role of the Social, Cultural And Environmental Structure of The Tribal Communities In Indian Sports

Tarak Mohan Hazari: Ph.D. Research Scholar, Dept. Of Anthropology And Tribal Studies, Sidho Kanho Birsha University, Purulia

Dr. Sudip Bhui: Assistant Professor, Dept. Of Anthropology And Tribal Studies, Sidho Kanho Birsha University, Purulia

Dr. Sanjay Kumar Chouhary: Cultural Administrator and Social activist

Introduction

Indian civilization is one of the oldest civilisations in the history of the world. And the biggest reason for the survival of this civilization for so many years is its uniqueness. The socio-cultural environment of Indian civilisation is very rich from ancient time. The continuation of which is still present. And among the various elements of this vast cultural heritage, sports is one of the most significant. it is known to all that sports have been one of the most entertaining aspects of human society since ancient times.

Religion is an essential identity of ancient Indian culture, and therefore many physical sports are influenced by religion. Various seals and some other artifacts have been discovered in the Indus Valley which proves that boxing and hunting started then. Different sports are also described in various mythological stories. Among them, the dice game of Mahabharata's or 'Pasha Khela' is one of the most notable examples. It was not an ordinary game, it had to do with important issues like the politics of the time and the usurpation of the throne. In the history of ancient India, the game of polo was widely practiced during the 'Sultani period'. What we call modern archery today was once part of hunting, one of the most popular sporty activities in ancient times. The popular game Chess also came from India, where it was formerly called Chaturanga.

The most primitive inhabitants of India are the tribal communities of India. As a result, they have witnessed different periods of social, political and cultural changes in India in the course of time. Naturally, it is not impossible for them to be familiar with many ancient games of India. And their hardworking bodies and mindset make them quite proficient at any ancient sport. So, the participation of tribal communities in Indian sports is very significant. The tribals of India are still one of the most deprived communities in India. Still, they have to struggle constantly to survive in this independent India. Naturally, their daily struggles help them to develop a more playful mindset. Their socio-cultural environment and their structure play a very effective role in their sporting decision-making. Indian tribes mostly live in hilly or forested areas, where they have to walk miles to get regular amenities. This not only makes them hardworking but also reflects mental toughness. The social system of these tribal areas drives the people through an unwritten practice of discipline, tolerance, and endurance of hunger and pain. This endurance helps them to excel in athletics. Also, the livelihoods of most indigenous communities have evolved to involve hunting and food gathering. As a result, an eternal tradition of confronting the enemy is ingrained in their blood. Also, they engage in collective activities, from repairing their houses to working in the paddy fields, which is another reason for making their sportsmanship mindset.

As per the Census of 2011, there was 10,42,81,034 Scheduled Tribe population in India which constitutes 8.6 percent of the total population of the country. The sex ratio among the Scheduled Tribes is 990 which was higher than the sex ratio of the total population (943). The Scheduled Tribes are notified in 30 states and Union Territories of India. The number of notified Scheduled Tribe communities in India is 705. There are 23 million tribal households in India. In West Bengal there are 40 enlisted Scheduled Tribe communities, although the number of individual tribal groups is 47. among them, santal is the largest community. The tribal inhabited areas of India are mainly spread over the states like Odisha, Madhya Pradesh, West Bengal, Chhattisgarh, Jharkhand, Maharashtra, Gujarat, Rajasthan, and parts of the North Eastern region. There are also many backward and underdeveloped areas among them. Yet over the years, athletes from the region have represented their respective disciplines at various levels. Even in today's India, many successful athletes have come from tribal backgrounds and continue to inspire hundreds of youngsters from different parts of the country to make a name for themselves in various sports.

The Story Of The Tribal Warrior Eklabya

Hindu mythology also could not avoid describing the skills of tribal people. At that time, the caste-based social system, despite having merit, the tribals was always deprived. Because at that time, who will perform the duties of society was determined by his community. Similarly, a deprived tribal warrior was Eklavya. According to the Mahabharata, Ekalavya was a young Nishad (a clan of hunters) prince. Being the son of the chief of hunters in the forest of Hastinapur, he aspired to become a very great archer and a brave warrior. Eklavya went to Gurudev Drona to learn martial arts. But Drona refused to accept him as a disciple as Eklavya was not a Kshatriya. But the boy Eklavya followed Drona as his guru and continued to learn martial arts single-mindedly in the forest. He made a statue of Drona and started his sadhana there. Once he achieved skills beyond imagination. When the news of his success reached Dronacharya, Drona immediately went to Ekalavya with Arjuna. Eklavya was overjoyed to see the Guru standing outside his room. Amazed at Eklavya's success, Drona does not understand anything and asks Eklavya when he taught Eklavya these things. Ekalavya points to the statue of Drona and says, 'I always feel that you are guiding me. You have not accepted me as a disciple, but in my eyes, you are my only teacher.' Drona is unable to break out of his narrow-mindedness when he sees how the intense pursuit of a Sudra man can take his talent to such heights. Then he made a trick to get out of his mental trap. He asked Eklavya for Gurudakshina. Asking Gurudakshina means that he is finally acknowledging Eklavya as a disciple. Thinking that he will be his disciple today, Eklavya promises to fulfill any wish of Drona with a simple mind. Then the drone looked for Eklavya's right thumb. The promising student keeps his word even though he realizes the teacher's trickery at the last moment. And Drona goes back thinking he has subdued Arjuna's potential rival. These stories of mythology prove that the indigenous people of ancient India were also quite skilled in sports and warfare. And that continuity is still present.

Historical Fact Of The Worlds Sports

In the ancient Sumerian civilization, there were sports such as Malla war, fist fights, running, tug of war, jumping, swimming, etc. Historians believe that Many of these games were also practiced in the Indus civilization of India. Chinese civilization originated various physical self-defense sports, presently which is known as "martial arts". However, among the ancient civilizations, the greatest development of sports took place in the Greek civilization. In 776 BC the Olympic Games started in Olympia, Greece. Various sports such as running, jumping, discus or javelin throwing etc. were organized here.

Later, after the collapse of Greek civilization, the Roman Empire spread over the world. This political pot change had a huge impact on the field of sports. At that time, different tastes and cultures were introduced into the world of sports. But the effect of violence in these games is very noticeable. An example is a gladiator fight in the amphitheater, where a slave had to fight in front of a hungry tiger. Some historians think that the game of football with a broken head started in this Roman civilization.

Then from the 16th century, various countries of Europe especially England and France established colonies in different parts of the world and tried to introduce their country's games. At that time, the British introduced to cricket, football, etc. in India by taking advantage of colonial rule. The British made sports compulsory in educational institutions in India. Its main objectives were two- (a) to civilize Indians through sports and (d) to keep the Indian youth away from nationalist movements through sports. But later, these sports assumed a huge role in India's freedom struggle. But as a result, the ancient indigenous games of India are almost on the way to extinction. Some of the most popular sports in India today are Cricket, Hockey, Table Tennis, Badminton, Carrom, etc. All of these were adopted by the British in colonial India.

Review of Literature

India is home to a diverse population playing various sports across the country. The history of sports in India dates back to the Vedic period. Physical culture in ancient India was fueled by religious authority. Many of today's popular games were born in this India. Badminton probably originated in India as an adult version of a very old children's game known in England as battledore and shuttlecock, the battledore being a paddle and the shuttlecock a small feathered cork, now commonly known as a "bird". Games like chess (chaturanga), snakes and ladders, and card games originated in India, and it was from here that these games were sent abroad, where they were further modernized. The founders of the Olympic concept had India very much in mind while deciding on various issues. Greece and India have an interesting connection that stretches back to 975 BC. Chariot rides and wrestling were common in both countries. But Indians have to struggle a lot when it comes to sports. Cricket is currently the most popular sport. Football is a popular sport in several states of India. Kabaddi is an indigenous game popular in rural India. Several sports originated in India, including chess, snooker and other regional games. India has won medals in Badminton, Kabaddi, Hockey and many other sports and disciplines. Cricket is most played after badminton and football. Besides cricket being the most popular sport in India, other popular sports are badminton, football, tennis, hockey and kabaddi. Also, India hosts several major events related to Tennis, Badminton, Hockey etc. (Malkappagol, 2018)

Sport is a very prominent social institution in almost every society, as it combines the characteristics found in any institution with a unique appeal. Sports are variously related to the processes of socialization and social change of different subjects. But the role of sports in not only social but also international relations and national development is immense, which dramatizes the political meaning of many societies. While the sport may be integrative at higher political levels, it has not been at the interpersonal levels of gender and race. The inequality that characterizes gender and race relations in society can also be found in sports. (Frey and Eitzen 1991)

Sports are actually a part of a society's culture and the development of sports is limited by the politics and economy of a particular community. It essentially acts as a catalyst and brings people together and influences social relationships as teammates working toward a common goal. Similarly, sports and physical activity reduce stress, improve sleep quality and prevent disease. Also, it is helpful in the therapy of several chronic diseases. Also, sports refers to a conscious and organized social activity that uses fundamental means to improve the human body, and overall human development, enrich social and cultural life and promote spiritual civilization. Also nowadays sports have started to emerge as one of the most powerful weapons of globalization and thus it can help people all over the world to know each other and push the process of globalization towards peace. (Bahir, 2020)

There is discussed about the published material on the traditional body and movement culture and modern sport as it was practiced in present-day Kenya from the time of first contact with whites until independence

(1963). At that time, all the sports that were in vogue became an effective weapon against colonialism until the 1950s. If Kenya had not been exposed to such influences at that time, the positive effects of sports would probably have remained more obscure today. The importance of sports as a medium of communication between whites and Africans was immense. (Mählmann, 1988)

Santals are the main tribe of West Bengal. They constitute about 50% of the total tribal population of the state. The other two major tribes are Oraon and Munda. These communities have more exposure to education and are more aware of various schemes and facilities for tribal people. In various sports organizations, Oraons are in majority (45.45%) followed by Santals (37.76%), while in districts Santals are in majority (55.56%) followed by Munda players (19.44%). This may be because these three tribal groups have more exposure to sports. Hill tribes like Bhutia, Tamang and Lepcha also involve themselves in various mainstream sports like football, archery, and karate.(Chowdhury, Chanda & Bej, 2018)

The relationship between African football and their European counterparts is actually a relationship of exploitation, mainly because of this world system theory. As the core countries dominate global sports and maintain their dominance by creating a global sports relationship that ensures discriminatory treatment. The globalization of sports in contemporary times has exacerbated that disparity and furthered the migration of talented African footballers to northern countries. Therefore, the relationship between nationalism and sports in the African continent is under serious threat. (Onyishi & Okou, 2016)

Significance of The Study

A country of diverse ethnicities, India's vast cultural heritage carries various streams. Among those cultural activities, ethnic and traditional games are very important in different parts of the country. Because sports have been one of the means of leisure and entertainment since ancient times. But they were not only games, they were one of the mirrors of the social life of that time. Among these games were several traditional games of various tribal communities. It is important to know how those ancient games influenced their social life and their participation in modern sports over time. Scheduled Tribes constitute a significant portion of India's population and many tribal players are currently involved in mainstream sports and games. In that case, how their socio-cultural structure helps them engage in sports is an important part of sociological research.

Apart from the participation and success of tribal players in sports in modern India, the main significance of this study is to analyze the social structure of three tribal communities namely Santal, Bhumij and Munda and discuss how they influence their ethnic representation.

Methodology

This study is mainly based on secondary data like Books, Websites, journals, Social Media, News Paper, Youtube videos etc. But, there are collected a few primary data through Interviews and phone call. This is a descriptive study, therefore the present study is qualitative in nature. This study is mainly based on three communities, Santal, Munda and Bhumij The method of sampling to choose the community is basically simple random sampling. The history of sports, their evolution, the tradition of sports in India etc. are reviewed from various articles and other sources and here discusses in detail of their relationship with the social life of tribal communities in India.

Remarkable Sportspersons of Tribal Community of India

Along with other communities in various fields of Indian sports, tribals have also shown considerable achievements and skills and are still striving for greater success. Some of the talented players who have contributed to Indian sports based on the socio-cultural and environmental situation of the tribal communities in different regions of India are Jaipal Singh Munda (Hockey), Bhaichung Bhutia (Football), Mary Kom (Boxing), Komalika Bari (Archery), Thonakal Gopi (Marathon), Birendra Lakra, Lalremsiami and Dilip Tirkey (Hockey)

Example of Traditional Tribal Games of India

There are many examples of indigenous traditional sports. All those sports are played both indoors and outdoors.Generally, the indoor games are played by young girls, boys and women in tribal areas. Bagh Chagol(Tiger & goat), Churi Khela (games played with bangles), Bou-Bor Khela (bride & groom game), Guti-Pathar Khel (games played with small stones), Khapti/Khapara Khel (games played with broken pieces of earthen pots), Ikir Mikirkhela, Kumbha-Ghar khela, Pemptibana Khel (trumpet making game), Lulukbana Khel (ornament making game), Puchi Khel, Kuhuluka (Blindfold game), Kadal-majha (banana plant), , Ghas Khel (making household instruments from different types of grass) are the some names of traditional indoor games played by tribals.

On the other hands, playing outdoor sports requires a wide field and open environment. Places like playgrounds, shade of big trees, harvest fields, or in some cases water bodies are preferred places for playing outdoor games. But generally, most of these outdoor games are mainly played by male people. In some cases unmarried girls also participate.

Some examples are Bhejabindha (archery), Kanamachi, kukudauda (catching a flying chick), kukudaladhei (symbolic cock fight), Haribhanga (breaking an earthen pot with blindfold) etc. Sometimes fishing, swimming, etc. also fall under the category of games. Children often enjoy playing khaparkati by throwing potsherds (broken pieces of pottery) on the surface of the water. Newly married couples throwing mud at each other is another popular water sport among some tribal communities.Bengali poet Jasimuddin wrote while describing the sweetness of villages traditional games.......

"Khela Moder Gan Gaoya Vai, Khela Langol Chosa
Sarata Din Khelte Pari, Janie Neko Bosa"

That means Singing, plowing is our sport. We can play all day for these, we forget to sit down. Such is the relationship of the sport with the traditional village life of the people.

Finding &Discussion

The ancient past and traditions can be explored by studying the history of various sports. Folk culture researcher of Bangladesh Dr. Ashraf Siddiqui has shown that the characteristics of tribal society are similar to the games of rural Bengal. Among the several games, namely 'Hadudu', 'Gollachhoot', 'Baghbandi' etc. reflect the tribal social life in alliances and groups. From this it can be understood that the tribal society had a deep connection with the rural areas of Bengal. In tribal contexts, games and sports are in many ways tied to their lifestyle, environment, culture, resources, and contact with the outside world.

Aboriginal sports are an integral part of their culture and one of the oldest forms of social interaction. Common features of tribal games are agreed upon rules, competition, element of fiction, element of chance, element of environmental concern, element of ritual, element of social work, set goals and personal enjoyment. Tribal games and sports capture the ideas and worldviews of their culture and transmit it to the next generation. Games were important as cultural and social bonding events, and some games were imbued with mythological and ritualistic religious significance. Traditional games were not just games, they were planned in such a way that they developed logical thinking, sensory skills, aim and concentration, basic maths, different sights and smells. Many skills like recognition, hand-eye development were developed. Many of today's modern games originated from these traditional games.

- Tribal games reveal various expressions of everyday life

"Rannabati" is a cooking game mainly played by both boys and girls between the ages of five and eight, which portrays their culinary heritage. In this game, participants prepare various food items symbolically in the guise of the game. They use different leaves and stems to make this dish. Cooking utensils are made from coconut shells. Also comes the image of selling various products through 'Hatbika' or marketed games. Here both boys and girls symbolically sell and buy various vegetables, food items, ornaments, clothes, utensils and other things, which they have seen in the market near them.

- These games evolved as an expression of rituals and rites of the tribal community

Adivasi children also imitate the law of animal sacrifice by catching some insects and sacrificing them in a symbolic act of their worship while playing. Which is actually a reflection of their social life.

- Traditional games serve as a means of spreading their social cohesion

Participants in tribal games learn socialization, friendship, cooperation, unity, discipline, social order and rules from the performance of various games. Aboriginal children learn successful application of skills and imitative knowledge from their games. Thus traditional games have a great educational value that teaches proper behavior, friendship and cooperation. These games act as a bridge between the past and present of the tribal society. These games instilled courage and endurance in the minds of the tribals, inculcating the tendency to use justice with their opponents. Team sports integrate individual interests and create habits of responsible cooperation towards collective interests.

- Tribal sports play an important role in spreading education

The process of education and socialization is completed through the practice of rural sports or folk sports. Social norms, beliefs and values are established in the process of play, thereby maintaining social balance. The importance of folk sports is immense in the adaptation of society to individuals. Among their various sports, they learn to build houses and do housework from some games. A game makes them clear about farming. Again there are games, from which the participants gather a good knowledge about flora and fauna.

However, climate and weather are not the same in all regions of India. As a result, the needs and desires of people change according to different places. And this dependence becomes the regulator of cultural heritage. And so the prevalence and popularity of the sport is not the same everywhere in India. For example, although the game of cricket is so popular all over India, the people of North East India have no affinity for cricket. The tribal dominated states of Central East India have produced many sporting talents who have played at various levels, from the state level to the national and international levels. In most cases, it has been observed that tribal players from certain regions excel in certain sporting events. For example, the massive participation of tribal youth from various districts of Odisha's Sundargarh and Jharkhand in hockey at national and international sporting events creates an impression that hockey is the sport of choice for tribals in these states. On the other hand, a similar pattern can be seen in wrestling and weightlifting among the North-Eastern tribals. This study mainly deals with three tribal communities, Santal, Munda and Bhumij.

Santal Community

Santal is the third largest tribal community of India . Santali is their mother language, this language belongs to the North Mundari Group of languages which is a part of the Austroasiatic Language Family.Santals also intorduce themselves as 'kherwal'. they are one of the hardworking community of eastern india. Generally they et up their villages in a hilly region or a high place near a forest or a river. In settlement, they attach great importance to the preservation of tradition as well as visionary intelligence. So almost all their villages have wide roads from one point to another point. And this road is well maintained, so that vehicles carrying wood from the forest or crops from the fields can move easily.The houses of them are built with mud walls and straw roof. On the entrance or out side the village there is a Teakgrove- that is called Jaher Than. Worships are done here in the name of Marang Buru, Jaher Era and other deities. Another important place is Manjhi Than'. This is situated near the house of the village chief or 'Manjhi'. They believe that the souls of four generations of Manjhis' or the first settlers in that village live there.

Santals are one of the very hardworking tribal community. And once they lived in quite remote areas and still they are living easily in some remote areas. They have not yet allowed their cultural heritage to be lost in the face of modernity. In that prevailing tradition, hunting still falls within their economic occupation. But not only for economic reasons, but at the same time it is one of their most enduring cultural molecules. Every year hunting festivals are held in different areas.

Their daily living helps a lot in creating a sportsmanlike mindset. The habit of sleeping early at night and getting up early the next morning to do their work keeps their body strong and fit enough. This physical fitness is the biggest sign of their mental health. And this stress-free life is very necessary for any physical activity.The biggest festival of Santals is Saharai. A very essential step of this festival is 'Cow Khunta'. in which traditional way this program is carried out looks a lot like boxing.

Their fearless and spontaneous participation in the hunting festival proves that they are quite capable of dealing with the enemy in any situation and at the same time they are quite adept at targeting. Keeping a cool mind under pressure is an integral part of any game. Also, the way their village head is elected through their traditional political system is actually quite similar to choosing a team leader or captain of a team.

Munda

Munda is the another notable tribal community of eastern india. they mainly inhabit in the region of Chotanagpur platue. they are well spread in the states of Jharkhand, West Bengal, Chhatisgarh, Orissa and Bihar. Munda generally means headman of the village.Anthropologists speculate that Munda was the first to establish a rural society based on equal rights in India. They always maintained their individuality in terms of land ownership or social customs. Before British rule no organization could interfere in their social system. Originally the head of their society was called Munda' - gradually the whole community came to be known as Munda.Perhaps the word Munda comes from the Sanskrit word mundo, meaning head. The origin of the Mundas is traced to the Proto-Australoid tribes of Chotonagpur, called Mura' or Horobans'. According to anthropologist S C Roy, the -Mundas originally inhabited North West India. After the Aryan invasion they took refuge in Azamgarh. But they could not stay there for long. They left Azamgarh and came to Chotonagpur. The region was surrounded by hills and full of forests. They cleared the forest and settled first. According to Munda custom, families who settled by clearing forests owned land jointly. They were called 'Khunt Kattidars', they allotted a fixed plot of land to each family. In this way the village of Munda came up in the Chotonagpur forest area by the "Khunt Katti"method. As a result of the change of this "Khunt Katti" system in the British rule, a new revolution in the history of India took place. The British Company dominated the Munda region, abolishing the traditional customs of the Mundas and establishing private ownership of land. It also introduced the rule of payment of rent in cash instead of grain. As a result, the Mundas became very angry and declared a rebellion against Sashak, which has been remembered as the Munda Rebellion in the history of India's freedom struggle.They enjoy their lives during various communal rituals, group hunting of wild animals and birds with bow and arrow, group dancing and singing and drinking native liquor irrespective of age at any function or festival.

Mundas are highly organized and shrewd. The social life of Mundas is much more organized than others. Politically they are quite skilled and savvy. And they are also very skillful in hunting. This well-rounded social life helps them tremendously in team sports. There are several traditional game of them. Most of them are now practiced in Jharkhand. Among them Phodi, Khati, Kouri-Lnu, Sim Sim, Kan kotra, Bikhai birki etc. are very prominent. Fodi is a type of tribal hockey in which the Mundas are most proficient. Another dramatic game of the Mundas is the jackal game (kantara-inu), which combines entertainment with education. Where children take on roles and create situations from real life. It revolves around a jackfruit. The game is played through thieves stealing fruits, cutting down trees and various other episodes. Jaipal Singh Munda is a shining star of the sports world of the Munda community who has left his mark of versatile talent in British India. Also worth a mention is Prakash Rameshwar Munda, who is the first cricketer of tribal origin to get a place in the Jharkhand Ranji team.

Bhumij

The term Bhumij denotes one who is born from the soil, Cultivation is the main economic basis of their livelihood. Also daily labour, collection of minor forest produce, animal husbandry, leaf plate sewing, hunting, fishing, petty trading etc. are also some of the economic activities of their daily life. The Bhumiji people are one of the primitive tribes who have lost their traditional cultural identity under the influence of Aryan civilization and have been and continue to be influenced by Hinduism. According to M Risley the Bhumij tribe is a branch of the Mundas: while spreading in the eastern side, they were mixed up with the Hindus and became separated from the main stream. They are belong to proto-Australoid by the origin of race.

They mainly live in West Bengal, Bihar, Jharkhand and in some cases Odisha. But their most remarkable feature is that they live scattered in different places instead of being united. Along with their cultural heritage, their own mother tongue is almost lost. Now they use the language of the region where they live. Once the Bhumij dialect was a branch of the Mundari language group, but at present they have almost forgotten that language. Now, they have become multi-lingual and are conversant in local languages like Odia, Hindi and Bengali.

But one advantage of Bhumij in this case is that they are fairly close to modernity. As a result, they make the most of the opportunities they get as adivasis. As a result, they are slightly ahead economically. As a result, they may come in contact with modern sports sooner. However, the social cohesion of the Bhumij is somewhat less than that of other tribals, in which case their group mentality is hindered to some extent. Some examples of games they participate in are Kan kotra, Bikhai birki, Chakidar (laughing game), Bicin, Kati.

Present status and problems

Although the economic value of sports in India is gradually increasing, the sports coaching institutes of the country are very indifferent. Since most of the tribal players are from poor economic backgrounds, they do not get the proper nutrition required for their sport, much less the equipment. Many subsequently withdrew as they did not provide the necessary kit and accessories. Many a times players face the problem of finding a suitable coach. Due to economic reasons, they gradually lag behind in mainstream team sports like cricket, football, hockey, kabaddi etc. Even if they participate in individual competitions like archery, athletics, gymnastics etc., they face difficulties at higher level. Again, due to the need of a lot of money to take these examinations, many qualified children fall behind.Beside it, awareness rate among the students of tribal community in schools level is very low regarding sports programs in various states, which is affecting sports talent and their parents' decision to choose sports as a career. Lack of awareness often leads them to wrong and sometimes misleading information. Despite the commercialization of sports in recent decades and special sports quotas in government jobs, the position of India's indigenous people at the highest level of sports is undoubtedly a cause for concern.

Conclusion

Inside folk sports there is a glimpse of life, a hint of society and history. And their exterior has been enriched by the proximity of nature, the influence of folklore, magic and religion. The activities of daily life, embellished with passion-conflict-loss-gain-happiness-pain, are translated into folk-plays in their own language and rhythm. Many precedents of the ancient history of human civilization are spread in different branches of culture. Past experiences are not rare in ancient folk games either. Some parts of these ancient histories have been transformed into sports in all these games. Similar glimpses of social symbols such as slavery, women abuse can be seen in folk sports. Since ancient times, sports have played a special role in the development of Indian society. An attempt has been made to understand the social structure of sports in different periods in India to highlight the evolution of sports in India. Viewed on a social scale, sports also bring people together and create a sense of unity among them. This rich history of sports is an important part of India's cultural heritage. Many games have evolved over the years, many have become extinct and many are still practiced in this country. Sports or physical exercise has occupied a very important place in the tradition of Indian tribal society since ancient times. Governments and various organizations dealing with sports should preserve and promote the endangered indigenous sports for generations to come, unite those people and instill a sense of pride in the cultural roots of a society. Therefore, emphasis should be placed on the preservation and appreciation of traditional and indigenous sports to maintain regional and national cultural heritage continuity.

Reference

Bahir, H. (2020) The Role of Sports on the Development of Tribes Unity: Afghan Society,Kabul, Afghanistan. American International Journal of Social Science Research. 5 (3)

Chowdhury. S. C. Chanda. A. Bej. V. (2018) Participation Of The Scheduled Tribe Players In Mainstream Sports: A Study In West Bengal. The Eastern Anthropologist 71: 3 & 4

Baskey, D. (2002) The tribes of West Bengal, Subarnarekha, Kolkata.

Eitzen, D. S., & Frey, J. H. (1991). Sport and society. Annual Review of Sociology, 17(1), 503-522.

Robers, Jhon M., Malcolm J. Arth and Robert R Bush, 1959 "Games in Culture", American Anthropologist, Vol. 6, No. 4, PP. 597-605.

Bandyopadhyay, K. (2005). Sports history in India: Prospects and problems. The International Journal of the History of Sport, 22(4), 708-721.

Washington, Robert E. and David Karen (2001) "Sport and Society", Annual Review of Sociology, Vol.27, PP. 187-212.

Mählmann, P. (1988). SPORT AS A WEAPON OF COLONIALISM IN KENYA: A REVIEW OF THE LITERATURE. Transafrican Journal of History, 17, 152–171. http://www.jstor.org/stable/24328696

Gulia, S. Dhauta, R. (2019) Traditional games in India: Their origin and status in progressive era. International Journal of Physiology, Nutrition and Physical Education 4(1): 1252-1254

Roy, A (2017) GAMES & SPORTS IN ANCIENT INDIA. International Education & Research Journal. Vol. 3(5). PP 607-609.

Onyishi, A, E. and Okou, T, F. (2016) Underdevelopment Of Sports In Africa, Or Africa In The Era Of Underdevelopment: A View From The Global South. International Journal of Innovative Research and Advanced Studies (IJIRAS). Volume 3 (12).

Bourdieu, P. 1991 "Sport and social class". In C Mukerji, M Schudson (ed.) Rethinking Popular Culture: Contemporary Perspectives in Cultural Studies. Berkeley/Los Angeles: Univ. Calif. Press.

https://www.upgradeyourself.in/2018/12/madhyamik-history_96.html

https://ir.nbu.ac.in/bitstream/123456789/1658/11/11_chapter_07.pdf

Reflection of Primordial Consciousness among Transformed Religious Life among the Santal Community of Purulia District

Dr. Sudip Bhui: Assistant Professor (Stage-III), Department of Anthropology and Tribal Studies, S K B University, Purulia, West Bengal, bhuisudip@gmail.com

Mr. Tarak Mohan Hazari: Doctoral Research Scholar, Department of Anthropology and Tribal Studies, S K B University, Purulia, West Bengal

Abstract:

Religion plays a pivotal role in socio-cultural life of people. Community specific behaviours reflect in traditional beliefs, worldviews, cognition, language, rituals with symbolic meaning and expressions. The entire components maintain harmony. Mobility among people is increasing with rational and technological development. Culture contact induced factors like educational, religious institutions attract people to go for gradual transformation. These phenomena affect different aspect of life. In this article authors have made an endeavor with a comparative study between a habitation nearby Puruilia district town and remote rural area. These two study areas are inhabited by Baptized Santal community. The research objectives are covered in nature of existing religious behavior, degree of transformation in relation to traditional life and ritual practices.

Differentiation in perceptions among the studied people helped to make a categorization. This helps to understand entire perspectives. Researcher has utilized participant observation, case study, and focus group discussion for data collections. Data interpretation has been made with making comparative acounts along with an orientation of experiences of different similar social milieus. Changes and transformations are found in three phases like religious practices by worshipping, ritualistic performances and customs and festive time commensality. Rationalities and technology-based life style, life with impact of socio-cultural setting also play important role in differentiations. This approach advocates need of more intensive studies to understand the basis of culture behaviors. Special importance has given on communication between informants and neighbours tribal communities.

Key words: Converted Christians, Tribal religion, Culture contact, Peri-urban habitation, forest vicinity, techno social forces, cultural behaviors and communication

Introduction

People live in their worldview to interact with themselves and others. Religion generally act as guiding principles, creates images in unconscious mind. Culture contact is cause of social mobility. Social change may be resulted in conflict, change of ideology and religion.Religious texts of India depicts about the tribal people as inferior races but they never completely aloof from the main stream of civilization. Tribal people lived in isolated natures' lap in pre colonial India. Christianity had been introduced among them as agent of favorable condition for expansion of colonial era.

People believe that supernatural spirits are present in our world or environment and this is sacred, aesthetic. Religion plays a significant symbolic role in a people, group of people's life. When someone falls into danger in his / her life, that time they pray their god and get sprits of faith. It is a sentiment of people which come from ancestor life through psychologically, physically with religious objects. It is a man with god relationship and it brings interaction with other social communities with variety (Horton, R., 1960). Religion is changed by time and transforms faith, Practice one generation to another generation (Mandelbaum, D. G., 1966).

India is the most human-diverse country in the world. This is the country of coexistence of people of different races, religions, and castes. And as a result of the combination of all these people, India is the most culturally rich country in the world. Among all components of diversity, the tribal community is one of the important sections of India. Among these tribal populations, Santal is one of the largest tribal communities of India. They live in several parts of India but are mainly found in the eastern part of the Indian subcontinent. Also, Santal tribes live in neighboring Bangladesh. There are some differences in the practice of religion among the various tribal groups in India, but they are basically nature worshipers. The Santals are no exception. They are basically followers of the *Sarna* religion.

The Santals are one of the largest tribes of India, spread over a wide area in eastern India like Jharkhand, Bihar, Orissa, and West Bengal. Some of them also migrated to Tripura, Assam and Bangladesh as plantation laborers in the tea gardens. They are racially Proto-Australoid (Guha, 1944). The Santals believe that, the world is a vast forum in which man/Women, spirits and impersonal forces are constantly in contact. Every people in their family, tribe live in local community along with in subcontinent must ensure its integrity and maintain harmony (Kerketta, 2018). The first attempt to convert the Santals to Christianity was led by the Protestant missionaries, the American Free Will Baptist Mission, in 1838. They were performing various welfare centric activities in the area along with their missionary work skillfully. With their influence the Santals were forbidden to drink rice beer and take part in the age old traditional dances. Not only that, they were told to stop playing the traditional musical instruments used during the dance. In fact, Christian missionaries viewed these dances as obscene along with free sex and drinking. Indeed, many Santals saw Christianity as a threat to their traditional society and a source of separatist power and loss of identity (Saha and Goswami, 2019). Before conversion, all members of the Santal tribe were class and socially equal. But after the conversion, a sharp distinction was made between the common Santals and the Christian Santals. Each of them tries to claim the superiority of his own 'religion' over the other and promotes various cultural and religious reasons to justify his attitude and evaluation. Due to the change of religion, the oral tradition of the Santals has been decaying and the influence of modern music is increasing in their life instead of their folklore and folk songs. And it is for this reason that Christian Santal children have entered the mainstream of education, with very few of them learning or knowing their tribal language (Jana, 2008).

Research Methodology

Literature review suggests the traditional life of Santal tribe in general and has been taken the period when all people were followed traditional religious practices. British missionaries came in the Santal Pargana and the Bihar state by adopting the means of social welfare. Culture contact, dissemination of western oriented knowledge of health care, religious curiosity brought elements to leave traditional life. But hypothetically, people cannot change themselves as community life in each and every aspect their age old life. The Santal people of Purulia district have had a series of cultural contact with the British but very few studies are available in these aspects. To trace the traditional practices interactions of people with nature, ritualistic life and material culture have been considered for tracing signs of tradition and transformed. As urban people are more mobilized than rural, segregation of transformation should be reflected in different degrees. In this study one village at distance of 5 kilometers from Purulia town and two villages at more than 28 kilometers from town and situated in less communicated area have been selected.

Pilot survey has been conducted for selection of fields; three villages are selected from more than ten villages. Structural and unstructured interview, participant observation, group discussions have been conducted with pre scheduled and after getting consent of informants. Case studies have been collected to authenticated and examine the special observation as cross section of community life related to specific issues.

Arm-chair anthropologists and ethnologists applied comparative methods to differentiate the evolutionary phases in different socio-cultural aspects. Radcliffe-Brown stated 'the comparative method does not only formulate problems, though the formulation of the right problems is extremely important in any science'. But this method is also very much effective in analysis of empirical research also (Radcliffe-Brown, 1958).

Comparative method is utilized to trace the primordial consciousness among the people under study. Apart from the Christian and non-Christian Santal people their social, cultural, aesthetics, media lives are also considered to understand process and degrees of transformation of traditional life with influence of different religious practices. Scheme of comparison has been made by traditional Santal religion (Sarna) and Christianity, socio-cultural life of Christian and non-Christian among Santal community, along with Christian Santal in rural and urban settings. Result of these comparisons is finally reflected in "Opening Zip" table.

Rational for the study

Study in social change is very common research in social sciences for understanding the transforming phases of socio-cultural phenomenon and policy level output to support human welfare. Peace studies are very much essential for contemporary world. Religion is the main perspective for peace from the time immemorial. Religion is also issue for violence in local and global interactions. In this paper local level scenario for dealing with religion in maintain of peaceful community life has been considered. Religious transformation among the tribal people in India is an age old issue of India but still matter of debate. Here researchers want to focus on dilemma of traditional or transformed religious identity is more sustainable for peaceful community life or compatibility remains with gradual transformation.

Objectives

This is the study to know about the past present and future of the Santal people who believed in Christian religion. Focuses of this study are covered in nature of existing religious behavior, degree of transformation in relation to traditional life and ritual practices. Differentiation in perceptions among the studied people helped to make a categorization. We have three objectives as following

a. To understand the relationship between religion and the rest of social life among the Santal tribe of Christianity in changing perspective of social-cultural life
b. To make comparative account of major aspects of socio-cultural life between peoples of traditional Santal religion and Christianity among the Santal tribe
c. To trace the present community cohesiveness against different forms of religious practices among Santal tribe in general

Community and the study area

Santal is the third largest tribal population of India and the largest tribal community in West Bengal. According to the census of 2011, there is total the population is 2,512,331. Their mother tongue is Santali, which belongs to the North Mundari Group of languages. Santali language is a part of the Austro-asiatic Language family. They have their own script called Olchiki, which was developed by Dr. Raghunath Murmu in 1925. Apart from Santali they also speak Bengali, Oriya, and Hindi according to their region. The Santal has 12 clans, each is divided into a number of subdivisions also based on patrilineal descent. A significant point here is that members of the same clan do not marry each other. A group of patrilineal clans like

Hansda, Murmu, Kisku, Hembram, Soren, Marandi, Tudu, Baske, Besra, Pauria, Charrey and Bedia has built their entire social structure, which is further divided into several khunt or sub-clans.Religiously, they follow the Sari or Sarna Dharam. But since that religion is not officially recognized, they often have to resort to other religions for various reasons. "Jaher Than" is the holy place for every Santal village where they perform their religious rites throughout the year.

Food habit is one of the important characteristics of any community. Here, Rice is their staple food. Besides it, they eat all types of vegetables and fruits. They also love to eat fish chicken or mutton. Haria (Rice beer) is a very popular drink among the Santals. Besides, they also drink *Mahua* liquor in some specific regions. Their social structure is very disciplined and strong. The social organization of them has a large flexible space not only for their own ethnic groups but also allows fraternity towards more than eight cohabitants tribes. Every ritual in a society like birth, death, marriage, etc., has its own rules, which is the manifestation of their nature-centered thinking. Equality is a very important part of their society. And so, every man and Woman in Santal society has equal rights. In the modern political system, it contributes in cast their vote and selection of candidate in nominating as public representatives.

Their economic life is mainly based on forests and agriculture; the identity of the traditional way of life of Santals found in various books and research shows that they were hunter-gatherers in the early stages of their cultural history. Hunting is still one of the most important occupations in different parts of the country. Then, with the passage of time, for various reasons, the ancestors of this ancient tribe gradually shifted their interest in horticulture and agriculture. Now they have become agriculturalists. The traditional economy of this tribe was composed of giving importance to the village as an economic unit rather than individual ownership with kinship based cooperation. They are rich in their traditional cultural heritage. Traditionally, the year for the `Santals' begins from the Bengali month `Magh' that corresponds to the month of February in English calendar. Throughout the year they involve in worshipping and perform rituals in festivals with changing nature of their environment. All these performances and thinking are indication of keeping sustainable nature offer a lesion to the rest of the world in prevent environment degradation.To grasp the traditional religious festival along with their calendar we may consider the following table:

Months	Festivals	Caring and worshipping objects
Magh	Maghmura,	Sal Tree, Pancha Bhut, medicinal herbs like Nilkantha, Anantamul, Shal mul, etc.
Phalgun	Baha,	Big Hill, Sal and other trees, conservation of animals
Baisakh and Jaistha	Ma More, Eroy Sim,	Things responsible for better Agricultural production
Asar	Asari,	Seedlings, plants of tree
Bhadra	Karam, 'Harier sim'	Germinations of seeds of crops

(Bhui, and Mandal, 2016)

The primary data of this study were collected from the three village of Arsha and Purulia I blocks of Purulia district. Name of the villages are Gandhabazar, Manguria and Harmadi. Among these villages, Gandhabazar and Harmadi situated at Arsha block and the distance between these two villages is 3 km. Manguria is situated at Purulia I block and a sub-urban area of Purulia town.

Harmadih is a medium size village located in Arsha Block of Purulia district, West Bengal. There live total 141 families. The village is mainly inhabited by three communities, Christian Santal, Non-Christian Santal and Kurmi. Total population of the village is 805 , out of 411 are males while 394 are females. Harmadi is situated at Banks of the Bandu river, which is one of the most important rivers of the Ajodhya hill area. The distance of Purulia town from the village is about 28 KM. It is notable that, most of the village population is from Schedule Tribe (ST). Schedule Tribe constitutes 68.08 % of total population in Harmadih village. Mainly there live two communities, Santal and Kurmi. Among the schedule tribe populations, all are the Santal. Christian Santal are of more families than the Non-Christian Santal.

Harmadi (Rural Setting)					
Age Group	Christian Santal	Non-Christian Santal	Kurmi	Others	Total
Upto 17	58	73	62	0	193
18 – 59	146	211	171	0	528
60+	24	31	29	0	84
Family	42	54	45	0	141

There are two churches present in this village. One is G.E.L church and another is Roman Catholic Church. The Christian population of the village is also divided by the rules of the two types of the church according to their religious belief. But the villagers celebrate together all the festivals. There is an interesting fact about the village. Local master Lahmia Marandi said in describing the incident "At one time 5 people lived in Harmadi village. Among them, now there are Christian Santals in the whole village, they are the descendants of only two of the five. The descendants of the other three have left the village long ago for some reasons.

Another village is named Gandhabazar. This is a medium size village located in Arsha Block of Purulia district, West Bengal. There are total 310 families residing in this village. It is basically a multi-community village. The most notable community of these multiple communities is Rajwar. The Gandhabazar village has a population of 1692 of which 857 are males while 835 are females. Among the population, most of the villagers are from Schedule Caste (SC) & Schedule Tribe (ST). Schedule Caste (SC) constitutes 63.64 % while Schedule Tribe (ST) was 32.96 % of the total population in Gandhabazar village. The village has another economic significance, as it is located on the road to the Ajodhya hills, the most popular tourist destination in Purulia. Sugarcane is one of the economic crops grown here. However, at present, the amount of sugarcane cultivation has decreased due to various reasons. There are live 5 families who belong to the Christian Santal community. The nearest hospital of those villages is Sirkakabad BHPC. The nearest College name is Arsha College. Tamna is the nearest railway station. Ajodhya hill, the most popular tourist spot of Purulia is very close to the two villages.

Gandhabazar (Rural Setting)					
Age Group	Christian Santal	Non-Christian Santal	Rajwar	Others	Total
Upto 17	14	83	213	70	380
18 – 59	31	224	735	215	1205
60+	5	21	64	17	107
Family	9	58	191	52	310

Besides it, there are also collected data from Uffmanpur hamlet of Manguria village under Purulia 1 block. Manguria is one of the nearest villages of Purulia town. Manguria is a very large village, divided into several parts or areas, Uffmanpur is a small part. It is also a multi-ethnic village. There is Hindu and Christian as well as Muslim populations. Looking at the communities, there live Bauri, Brahmin, Kurmi, etc. peoples of several communities. There are total 675 families residing in the village. The total population is 3808 of which 1949 are males while 1859 are females. The total literacy rate of Manguria village was 79.32 %, among this Male literacy is 89.53 % and female literacy rate 68.63 %. There are 809 Scheduled Caste (SC) and 267 Scheduled Tribe (ST) populations in the village. There live about 5 santal Christian families.

Manguria (Sub-urban setting)					
Age Group	Christian Santal	Non-Christian Santal	Bauri	Others	Total
Upto 17	9	21	84	796	910
18 – 59	17	39	266	1883	2205
60+	6	11	53	623	693
Family	5	13	76	581	675

Socio-cultural life and perspective of religious practices

Religion is one of the most important aspects of their life. Reason for conversion is an important point. The main reason for conversion towards the village is social but the main reason for the religious conversion in the urban area is very personal. This reflects differently. For example, the Santal Christians peoples in the urban area keep various pictures of the cross sign in their car or on the door of their house, which is rarely seen in the village. However, lately, this effect is gradually increasing in the villages as well. Although they are equally respectful of their own religious rites, towards the village they spontaneously attend various ceremonies of the common Santals, which the Christian Santals of the city do not usually do.

Ritual

The results of various studies show that there is a significant difference in the level of religious beliefs and rituals between rural and urban dwellers. Rural people have higher levels of faith and religious observance than urban people. Furthermore, among the sub-dimensions of ritual, there is no significant difference between rural and urban dwellers in intellectual religion alone. There is a significant difference in the level of religiosity of the total urban dwellers and the rural dwellers, and the level of religiosity of the rural dwellers is higher than that of the city dwellers (Nikkhah, 2015). Here, one thing is very noticeable in the case of wedding rituals. Although there is a touch of modernity in the urban wedding style, in the village, the traditional wedding style is still followed. However, there is no difference in the funeral rites.

Economy

Although there are many technological advances in Indian agriculture, most rural farmers do not know much about the use of such technology, mainly because of lack of information and training along with illiteracy. So, the economic life of the rural and urban areas is therefore completely different. The mainstay of the rural economy is still agriculture, while the Christian Santals of the urban areas are involved in a variety of economic occupations. This does not mean that the people of the village are not associated with the job.

Material culture

There are also several differences between their several cultural aspects. In this case, material culture is an important phenomenon. There is no difference between the two societies in terms of dress. However, women in rural areas still use traditional ornaments like traditional Santals peoples. The use of modern ornaments is more prevalent in urban areas. The type of their house is mainly depending on their economic situation. But in the rural area, their traditional houses are more common to see, which are decorated in various colors. This is the same as the traditional Santals community. Their food habits are almost the same in all the regions of surrounding but there is some variation in the festive season. For example, during Christmas, it is customary to eat cake in the town area, but it is more common to eat various types of traditional 'Pithe' in the village. This is one of the major differences in their food habits of them. Also, the people of the urban area cannot use natural things as easily as the people of the village can use them for various purposes, so they have to depend on the market for those things.

Since their population is relatively small, it is difficult to compare the lives of the two places as a whole. Moreover, in this age of globalization, rural public life is becoming more and more modern like the urban culture.

As a result, the difference in lifestyle between the two places is gradually decreasing.

Comparative account of Christian and Non-Christian Santal People

		Christian Santal	Non-Christian Santal
Marriage system		According to the Christian Marriage Act, both parties must be Christians. Rules and rituals are followed according to the Bible and Church authority along with senior of Christian groups monitor entire ceremony.	Following the rule of the marriage system of the Sarna religion. They have customary rules for marriage. Diverse rules are found. The marriage system is clan-specific.
		All the elements of observing the rules of marriage are derived from the market and easily available.	The majority of the elements of observing the rules of marriage are derived from nature. Different kins-man and relatives play specific role in collection of required materials.
		Marriage programs are organized in church. The decoration of this place is very simple and uniform ceremonies have to conduct.	Marriage programs are organized in the home. The place of the marriage is fully decorated in the traditional way.
Concept of Religion		Religious life is controlled by Bible. The true message of Jesus is preached through the church, giving instructions on how people should behave themselves in various ways. The most important and holy thing of the religion is Crush.	Religious life is basically oriented with nature. Ancestors, spirits are appeased with slide variations in their traditions. The most important and holy thing of the religion is Shal tree.
		The name of the religious place of worship is church. The Catholic church encourages to traditional practices of Santal community other than religion in orientation of western philosophy, culture, art, music, and science. The only god is Jesus. Besides, there is no other god here. The main festival is Christmas. Apart from this, there is no any religious festival.	The name of the religious place of worship is Jaher Than. The main deity is Marang Buru. But there are also several deities in the religion. Saharay is the main festival. Besides it, there are also several festivals.
		Their religion is followed in rational, liberal and reflexive social environment, individual personality are more acquainted with socio-religious system. People are more service oriented.	Animal sacrifice is inextricably linked with religious life. A hen is sacrificed before harvesting. Hunting festival is one of the important parts of the religious life.
Social life		There is no village organization. Everything in the village is controlled by the church. And the head of the church is the Father of the church. Church personal are careful to elevate educational, professional and communication development.	There are several important roles of village organization in social life. From this organization, various policies of the village are determined and social problems are solved. And the chief of the organization is called Majhi.
		Since the impact of education is high, social life is totally free from superstitions.	Due to illiteracy, social life is severely affected by superstition.
		Although there are clan divisions in this society, The priest of the church is elected according to the Christian rules, so the father of the church may not belong to the Santal community.	Santal society is divided into 12 clans. Among the 12 clans of the Santals, Murmu is the only priest clan.
		Women have freedom in everything in society. So, there is no practice of child marriage.	Society is still lagging behind in the question of women's freedom. Yet child marriages are performed at different times

Conversation

Religious conversion is special case to a particular religion but in course of foreign intrusion and colonial rule of India, we observe various reasons. In this field area we can found the different reasons for conversions which has been recorded from memory of informants.

1. Attracting towards the western religions due to frequent contact with missionaries

2. Convenience available to conversed people

3. Problems arises from marriage with mate outside of an ethnic groups promote to safe identity and status by conversion

4. Forced conversion by dominant groups as punishment of ritualistic malpractices, sorcery and witchcrafts

5. Conversions due to conversions of major kin and relative circle and avoid the marginal identity

There are many of the above factors are responsible for the converting of the Santal of Purulia district. Missionary activities of Purulia has had golden history in services to destitute like leprocy affected patients, poverty trodden tribal people, mitigation of inter ethnic violence they became integrated with the social life of the Santals. They paid special attention to the Santali language and literature for reformations. In fact, at that time the East India Company give them permission for missionary work. After failing in Calcutta and adjoining areas, they started their work by exploiting the simplicity of the tribals of the Chotanagpur region. In various ways, they converted the Santals into Christian. Many were forcibly converted, just as many were attracted to their religion and joined their religion. This tendency increased after the Santal Rebellion. It is noteworthy that, most of those who change their religion are extremely poor. Here it is notable that, at that time there were various rumours about the census, rumour was created due to their religious conversion.

There is one of the reasons for conversion is marriage. This is one of the interesting parts of their life. In a country like India, the marriage of a man and women of two different religions is not acceptable in most cases to society. All the Santal families who have converted to Christianity since the British period, at present any Santal have to convert to Christianity in order to marry someone from that Christian Santal family.

Another important reason for conversion is the superstition of Santal society. People in rural areas strongly believe in witchcraft. There prevails unrest in their society at different times. The poultry, cows, and goats of the suspected victim are often seized by village authority (dominant part in general) and there is also a possibility of his/her death by violence. Since, Christianity is completely free from superstition, in such a case; the Christian Santals encourage him/her to their religion and give him refuge. This is exactly the reason why two families in Harmadi village were converted, although they later returned to their religion. Poverty and poor health is other reasons for this change of religion for expectation to betterment.

Religious institutions among the Christian Santal

The church is the only place of worship in Christianity. Church is mainly two types, Catholic and Protestant. There are more subdivisions between these two. A Catholic is a Christian who is often associated with the Roman Catholic Church. They believe in the power of the popes, who follow the apostle Peter (the first head appointed by Jesus). Catholics believe in higher positions or positions of authority. They are the ones who use the images and pictures as a way to encourage. They believe Jesus was the son of God, receive Baptism, confess their sins, and take part in Holy Mass to obtain this. They worship Mary because they consider her as the queen of heaven. The word Catholic usually means 'universal'. On the other hand, A Protestant is a Christian known for protesting during the Reformation. They do not believe in the supremacy or authority of the pope. They opposed the church and pointed out a few errors. They do not normally use images as an incentive. They must believe Jesus was the son of God and that he has already paid the penalty for your sins to receive this. The word protestant usually means 'protest'. The protestant is divided into different groups.

There are two churches in these villages. Among them, one is G.E.L (Gossner Evangelical Lutheran) Church and the Roman Catholic Church. Although both seem to be places of worship for the Christian Santals, there are some differences between the two churches. G.E.L is a Protestant church. G.E.L Church in Chotanagpur and Assam is one of the major Christian Protestant denominations in India. It was established on 2 November 1845. It is one of the three Lutheran denominations in northeast India along with the Bodo Evangelical Lutheran Church and the Northern Evangelical Lutheran Church. On the other hand, The Catholic Church is the largest Christian church, with 1.3 billion baptized Catholics worldwide by 2019. It is the world's oldest and largest continuously functioning international organization, which has played a significant role in the history and development of Western civilization. All these churches are basically run by two divisions. One is the spiritual section and the other is the administrative section. In the case of the Catholic Church, the head of the spiritual section is called Father and the head of the Protestant Church is the Reverend. Under the leadership of them, all spiritual and religious activities are completed. However, if they are absent in any case, the most experienced person among the members of the church is given this responsibility temporarily. In that case, he took the help of the religious *Panjika* of the Christian religion (Raj & Dempsey, 2000).

Another section of the church is the Administration section. It is actually a council formed on the basis of the votes of the members of the church. These members receive membership mainly through the baptism of their society. it is a process by which they take the membership of their religion. This administrative section is known as the Church council. A Parish Council is made up of 10 such church councils. These Parish councils are governed by the Diocese Council. There are 5 such Diocese councils in India. Churches in Purulia are part of the South East Diocese Council. And the Central Council is at the top of all these Diocese councils. And in this way, the administrative unit of the church is controlled.

The Catholic Church in the village of Harmadi has no committee of its own. The entire church is controlled by the Catholic Father of Purulia. He comes at a certain time every month and does his work. However, one of the villagers has been given the responsibility of the church. He carries out all the daily activities, prayers, etc. For this he has been specially trained. However, another special feature of the devotees of this church is that they consider the born as sacred and also worship it. A total of 20 families in the village follow the Catholic Church.

On the other hand, the GEL Church of the village has its own committee. That committee changes on the basis of votes from time to time. There are a total of three committees. The main committee consists of 5 members, one of whom is the secretary and one cashier and the other three are general members. There are also women's committees and youth committees. A "Church Behera" has also been assigned to maintain the church. He was given a monthly stipend from that committee. And the money that is needed to run all these activities is basically collected from all the members of the church. There are a total of 22 families under this church.

About 30 years ago, a young Santal man from Harmadi village got into a lot of trouble due to water accumulation in his spine. At that time, the then Father of GEL Church personally helped him a lot. He even took him with his family to Bankura medical college. In this case, this father was greatly assisted by the local church committee. This fact reflects the coexistence of people of two religions in same village.

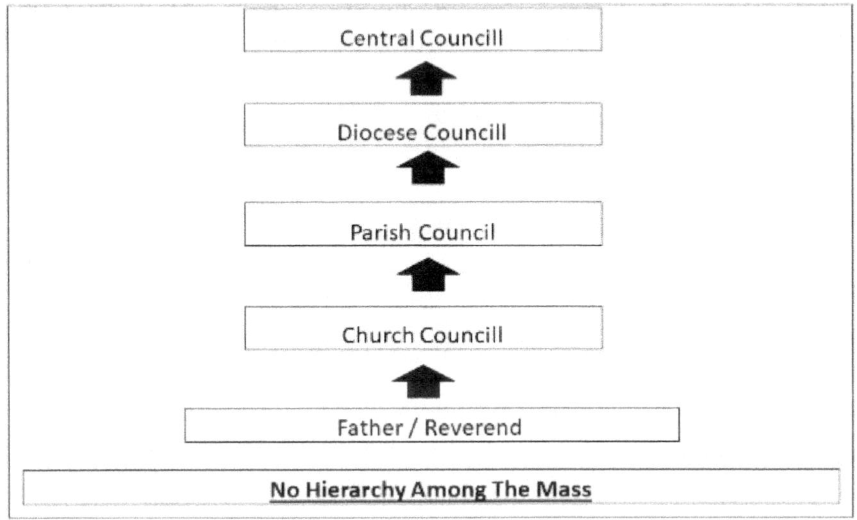

Socio-cultural life of Santal Christian people of Purulia district

Dress and ornaments

The dress pattern is one of the major identification marks of any community. There is nothing special about the dress pattern of the Christian Santal peoples. Men usually wear shirts and pants. At home, they wear *lungi or dhoti*. However, unlike common Santals, they do not wear any traditional dress. They celebrate any festival or event wearing a plain pants shirt or a simple dress. This is where they differ from the common Santals. Younger girls of their community wear frock or *Churidar*. Married women usually wear sari and blouses. They have no obligation to use vermilion like the Santal society. In this case, the preference of women is more important. Married women often use Kajol in their eyes. They don't use traditional jewelry at all; rather, they use light modern jewelry. When they are at home, they use two single bangles in both hands. The practice of tattooing is not common among Santal Christians, but there are no religious barriers to tattooing.

Marriage system

They follow the rules of Christian religion in their marriage system and so their weddings are usually held in the church. Here it is notable that, if there is no church in a village, then the marriage is solemnized at home if the two families agree. In this case, the financial condition is important. However, the use of the 'Crush' during the wedding is very noticeable. The bride has to wear a white dress at the time of marriage; on the other hand, although there is no color requirement for the wedding dress for the grooms, he has to wear a pants shirt during the wedding. Although in the case of home marriage, there is some similarity in their marriage system with general Santals. But the use of 'Crush' is not present in the marriage ceremony of General Santals. However, church marriage or home marriage in both cases, the presence of the Father of the Church is highly desirable. The groom's party is responsible for bringing that Father.

Religious belief

Religious belief of the Christian Santal community is very important and interesting. Although everything about the Santals is centered on nature, but the religious belief of the Christian Santals is entirely biblical. There is no place for superstition in the Bible, so all their customs are completely devoid of superstition. Superstitions are associated with most of the religious rites of Santal society, such as many Santal families' sacrificing a hen before harvesting their paddy and there are several examples like this. But nowhere in the Christian religion is superstition tolerated. When a member of the Santal community dies, he is either buried or cremated according to the wishes of his family. But there is no practice of cremation in Santal Christian society. If one of their family members dies, they have to be buried according to Christian rules. They perform their religious duties as they wish. But when it comes to celebrating, they celebrate together, whether it's Saharay or Christmas.

Thirty to thirty-five years ago, the Christian Santals of the Harmadi village participate in the "Gorukhunta" (cow irritation) program with the general Santals. Because then the population distribution was different, the population was much less. And the most important thing is that the celebration of the village was among the people of the village, because at that time no case was practiced, so they could participate without any hesitation. But now with the increase in population, they too have gradually withdrawn from direct participation. Now they did not perform cow irritation (*Goru Khunta*) ritual. Although there are some religious reasons behind this move, but the main reason is social.

Social system

The Christian Santal have no religious affiliation other than the church. As a result, their social life depends entirely on the church. Unlike the

Santals, there is no permission for arbitration. They do not have any posts like Majhi, Paranik, and Yoga Majhi etc. of the Santal community. So, if there is any social unrest, they solve it as they like, in this case, if there is no solution then they go to the church. Another important aspect of their social life is the freedom of women. Although the social system of Santal community also recognizes the freedom of women, in real life, many women do not get that freedom. But in Christian Santal society girls are given complete freedom at will.

But socially there is no conflict between these two groups of Santals, there is a friendly ralation. Many times, people of other communities deprive the Santals by use the opportunity of simplicity of them in various ways. For the same reason, they have been also tortured in various ways. There have even been cases of land grabbing by showing them false temptations. In this case, the Christian Santals have played a leading role in reclaiming those lands. There are many examples like this. Advancement of Christian Santal play savior role to entire Santal society in these cases.

Although the religions are different, the two communities are one in ethnic identity. So it is very natural that Santal Christians should have the identity of their ethnicity. So even though they have avoided the various religious festivals of the Santals from a religious point of view, they also celebrate them as they do. So they also show their artistic talents by the traditional wall painting on their own walls like the general Santal community. During the festival, different types of traditional 'Pitha' or bakes are also made in their house. They also drink traditional alcohol like 'Hariya' (Rice Beer) and 'Mohula' in celebration of the festival. The people of Santal Christian community actively participate in Santali dances also during festivals.

Education

Education was one of the most important part for the Christian missionaries when they tried to convert the Santal to the Christian religion. So, education is very relevant in changing the character from a traditional Santal to a Christian Santal. Because at that time they understood that if they could educate the illiterate Santals, half of their work would be easier. However, at present Santal society is also quite educated. But even then, the missionaries still continue to introduce their own education system for their society. That is why many schools were set up in different places, where only Christian boys and girls could study. The main purpose of establishing these schools was to enable Santal Christian children to be educated in the modern education. Holy Child School in Purulia is one such example. However, due to various government projects, they have reduced their benefits in the field of education in the last 10 to 12 years. But the Christian missionaries did not try to change the language of the Santal community, even though they asked to change their religion. So, they speak Santali fluently till now. It is an important step to save their racism.

Variations of Christianity in three studied villages

The location of the villages is very important here, as Harmadi and Gandhabazar are located about 28 km away from the district headquarters, while Maguria is the nearest village to Purulia town. These differences in position have influenced the observance of different customs and rituals in these villages. Due to its proximity to the city, the people of the Christian Santal community of Maguria have been heavily influenced by multiculturalism. There is also a difference in the celebration of their various festivals like Christmas. Two villages are located far away from the urban setting. And in that case, there are celebrate the festival in traditional way. On the other hand, the Christian Santals of Maguria are accustomed to modern life. So it is natural that there will be modernity in their celebration. Among the three villages, only Harmadi has two types of Christian Santal, Protestants and Catholics. But in the other two villages, only one type of Christian lives. There is no church in Gandhabazar among the three villages. They celebrate through the church in the Aharra village. Since there is no church in Gandhabazar, the Christian Santals there are at least somewhat deprived of missionary help compared to other villages.

Since the Santals have their own religion, the relationship between the two groups is very important. The relationship between the Christian Santals and the Santals in the village of Harmadi is very good, so they go out of their religious rites and celebrate many feasts with the Santals. But there is no such celebration in Gandhabazar or Uffmanpur.

Rural-urban differences among Christian Santal people

Religious life of the Christian Santal group is influenced by other congregations of social-cultural factors like nature closed rural life and globalization oriented urban life. Social cohesiveness in rural life exists in an integrated community and village-based activities. In these findings from field observation help to consider that primordial consciousness is reflected more among the rural Christian Santal people.

There are several differences between the urban and rural life of Santal Christians. Just as there is simplicity in rural life, there is modernity in urban life. In the case of education, the people of the town get a little more benefit than the people of the village. Also, there are a few more basic differences in other sections of their life. There are also several Santal Christian families in Ufmanpur village on the outskirts of Purulia town. The scope of their life is very different from the rural areas like Harmadi. They have frequent contact and common platform ritualistic life with the urban counterpart and attend church of Purulia town. Frequent participation religious discussion on Christianity and practical solution of many domestic solution led them rational thinking and competency in religious and social life.

ASPECT	RURAL	URBAN
Religious Practice	Santal Christians are on the committee of the village church, Since the village churches are controlled only by Santal Christians, they practice their own religious practices in those churches.	They do not get such benefits in the urban area church. Because the church in the urban area does not have the same rights as the village church of Santal Christians.
Social Ceremonies	They also attend various festivals of the neighbors. In the rural area, the traditional wedding style is still followed.	They usually do not attend the festivals of the neighbors. There is a touch of modernity in the urban marriage rituals.
Religious Festivals	During Christmas, it is more common to eat various types of traditional 'Pithe' in the rural areas	During the festive season, the cake is a common food to celebrate the season in urban life.
Economy	The mainstay of the rural economy is basically agriculture.	Christian Santals of the urban areas are involved in a variety of business and several economic occupations.
Language	Everyday life depends on the Santali language; they speak Santali with their family and neighbors. Even in church prayers, mantras are recited in the Santali language.	Although they are ethnically Santal, they speak more Bengali language than Santali language. Many of them do not even know Santali.
Material culture	Women in rural areas still use traditional ornaments like non-Christian Santals. The problem of the two neighbors is basically considered as an internal matter of the village, which is fixed by the people of the village. Because there is the strictness of social discipline in the village.	The type of house in the urban area is basically a pucca house. There is no reflection of tribal life on the wall of those houses. Women of the urban area used to like modern ornaments according to availability. if there is a quarrel between two citizens in urban areas, the police need to intervene.

Perceptions and expressions in childhood among the Christian Santal community

Childhood is early phase of human life. In rural area children are acquired their knowledge, information and experiences not by only elderly of their family or society but also as joint ventures of peer groups. These aspects of life sometime reflect their rural life also. Religion provides us perceptions about the dangers, uncanny facts and our thought beyond. In the following table we have examined that children of Christian Santal community have likely experiences with their traditional counterpart.

Age group		Fear	Explanation
Up to 10 years	Darkness	Fear of ghosts or fear of being attacked by any supernatural power	At an early age, Christian Santal children play with non-Christian Santal children. And at that time, they talk about different supernatural things about ghosts in different ways, and then everyone is scared when they hear that story. This fear is mainly due to their supernatural beliefs, which non-Santal children get due to their ethnicity and is transmitted to their playmate Christian Santal children.
	Remote place	Fear of getting lost or alone	Because of that fear, they do not want to be alone in a remote area. Because the same fear works in remote areas. Because during this time, Santals' traditional ideas about nature is transmitted to Christian Santals in various ways. In order to escape from that fear, Christian Santals often resort to the traditional way of life of non-Christian Santals.
11 – 18 years		The fears begin to subside. New knowledge about the nature is gained.	During this time, they were influenced by the teachings of the missionaries. Various aspects of Christianity began to influence life, rather than the ideas of non-Christian Santals. Religious consciousness is awakened.
19 and more		The Church became the foundation of all thought consciousness.	Religious customs are completely come into mastered. They maintain good relations with their neighbours but is not influenced by their words. As a result, all previous meditative ideas about nature changed.

The entire table is reflected in development of thoughts experiences about facts in which generally explanation come from religious perceptions and concepts. Early phase of the rural Christian Santal children also possess the like experiences of traditional Santal but gradually they differs from traditional to Christianity as their orientations have been made.

Various problems and solution in their socio - religious perspective

People have to face many problems in life. They cannot found proper reason for all the problems. Religion at its primitive form supported human to get some satisfactory causes and lead to practices rituals, worship and other performances. In this field area reflections of some experiences are found to mitigate and understand the critical health problems, accidental cases, natural calamities and supernatural facts.

Problems	Causes	What Have to Done
Various Disease/ Leprosy Etc.	1. Every human being commits some sin in life, so everyone has to suffer in different ways. 2. Continuing some bad habits, and not paying attention to minor physical ailments	1. The missionaries have various projects for this. Different programs are also taken on behalf of different churches.
Accidental Case	1. Because of disobeying the Lord, lying to the Lord, avoiding the Lord, etc. 2. Many of them feel that it depends on fate.	1. The patient does not always recover, he/she has to ask forgiveness from the Lord in these cases.
Supernatural	1. Most of these cases are of other religions, and these are often the main reasons for religious conversion	1. Congregational prayer to Jesus, service to that person by the church
Drought / Thundering	1. All of this is written in the Bible, These are the result of irregular use of natural things. 2. These are the laws of nature; man has nothing to do.	1. In these cases, the only way is to pray to the Lord according to the rule of the Bible. 2. Beside it, Man's behavior with nature must be corrected

Christian Santal people have less difference in perceiving the problems as supernatural and find explanations from their religious thought and practices. Both of different religious groups of Santal community express same causes for the abovementioned facts. Both make prayers to their Gods in different ways and with help of different religious experts.

Inter community relationship

Like the Santal community, they have not any specific village. So, they live with the other many religious communities like Hindu, Muslim etc. In particular, they live mostly with the general Santal community. Here it is notable that, in case of their own religious festivals, they observe their own rituals at their home but they celebrate together outside their home. For example, the Santal Christian people celebrate the 'Bandna' and 'Saharay' festivals by singing and dancing with them but they did not worship any cow in their house. However, they refrain from any kind of superstition and any program like animal sacrifice. On the other hand, they also invite others to celebrate their Christmas or Good Friday. But in the case of religious observances, they do not allow anyone.

Primordial state and transformation

Different aspects of socio-cultural life reflect the similarities and differentiations exist among the traditions and transformation through the following chart.

	Christian Santal	Non Christian Santal
Language	Speaking Santali in home and with relatives and also with the neighbours. Officially both classes are belonging in Schedule tribe.	
Living Pattern	Stay together, Participate in each other's various social programs. They actively participate in Santali dances during festivals. Both of them decorate their wall by their own traditional system and artistic mine.	
Relation with others	The people of the two communities help each other, whether it is a family affair or a danger to the villagers. There is a lot of evidence of this. Many years ago, a young Santal of the Sarna religion recovered from a spinal cord injury and recovered with the help of Christian Santals. This is the identity of the association of two classes of people.	
Food Habits	Staple food is rice, beside its various type of traditional food also be eaten. Although not everyone was involved in the celebration of the various festivals of the Santal community, at that time almost everyone celebrated the festival days by making cakes at home. They also drink alcohol like 'Hariya' (Rice Beer) and 'Mohula' (Fruit beer) in celebration of the festival.	
Food Habits	Both classes are heavily influenced by Western culture. This has led to many changes in language, eating habits and traditional way of life. The use of modern dress instead of traditional dress, higher education of girls, hospitalization when the body is sick, all these cases have changed a lot.	
Clan	There are clan divisions in this society, there is no difference between them. The priest of the church is elected according to the Christian rules, so the father of the church may not belong to the Santal community.	Santal society is divided into 12 clans. These tribes are basically divided on the basis of work. among the 12 clans of the Santals, Murmu is the only priest clan.
Religious belief	Religiously, they are the follower of Christianity, and so, animal sacrifice does not exist in the religious life. Religiously, various sayings of Jesus Christ are preached here.	Religiously, they are the follower of Sarna Religion, Animal sacrifice is inextricably linked with religious life. A hen is sacrificed before harvesting. The essence of this religion is nature-centered.
Marriage	Marriage programme are organised in church. The decoration of this place is very simple and decorated with modern decor.	Marriage programme are organised in home. The place of the marriage is fully decorated in the traditional way. No mantra is recited during marriage.

Conclusion

Religion is an aspect of life, the transformation of this aspect cannot bring entire change in short time. So, an arrow head change processes are observed in this field area. In the early days a small portion of the village people practiced Christianity in this respect all the villagers share more or less uniform social cultural life. In spite of religious practices villagers take part in fairs, festivals, especially the nature centric festivals like *Saharay, Baha*. They took part the traditional song, music and dances. In these three multiethnic villages of Purulia district Christianity play a diverse role in process of socio-cultural transformations. Catholic churches are more sensitive to traditional Santal religion, protestant (GEL) church are rigid against the traditional religious practices. Gradually Christian population increase and they take religious education from local church and major theological schools in Ranchi, in Purulia the eighties decade of last century Missionary schools also set up and bring the religious minded people. These educated and conscious people argue against the elderly to led proper baptized life.

At the preliminary phases process of transformation was confined to perception of God, conceptualization of religious thoughts and regular and ceremonial worshipping. After increasing the member of converted groups, getting thrust from education created more differences at the rituals related to worshipping like festivals, rituals performed at village units like possessions, group meeting. Then the next phase of transformation comes in invitations, interactions and group activities of social ceremonies. Customs related to ancestral worshipping, caring and proud making for animal and plant come after this phase.

Communication and living in social media play a very crucial role in making tendency of mobilization. In three or four decade's earlier radio, televisions were not available to majority of Christian Santal people they were guided by Church personals. But introducing of different gazettes and media people learned more about ideal religious practices of Christianity. Along with the religious lessons people also adopted the social life of Christianity across the globe. People are well connected through WhatsApp groups in different purposes. Members of this particular get more cohesiveness and feel proud about their ideal Christianity and earn stronger "we" feeling. This frames the concentric multi-circle zones in reference to ideal Christianity. Here the people less connected with e-media (rural counterpart) are carried more primordial content as community members and practice for conserve traditional life.

Still in present situations people speak in same language, though educated people use more English and Hindi words in Santali. Rationality and worldview reflected through language are varied from age to age of the villagers. Few people want to get explanation for coexistences of viewpoints when think about the social progress, environmental preservation, values embedded in language social ceremonies and non-religious behaviors to play role in maintain village solidarity. Art and aesthetics among the villagers are interpreted as their common intellectual property. Wall painting, Drama, songs and music with sense of social advancements like equality, women empowerment, and community pride provide common platform to remain united beyond the religious practices.

Recently dichotomy between Traditional and Christian Santal community are facing rising conflicts about their identity in political and administrative aspects. Many uprising and protests are observed in Jharkhand on "Christian Santal community left their traditional religion and they have no longer eligible to admissible benefits for Scheduled Tribe identity". Increasing diversions also will bring new perspectives of research in near future.

Present discourse of research advocates in search of peace keeping social cultural perspective, religion should be treated as natural entity and sustain upon the community centric decision making process in case of dilemma or conflict arises. Religion cannot be treated as separate entity but should be viewed as integrated part of entire gamut of society. Peoples' spontaneous involvement at grass root level interactions with their traditional solidarity will be more sustainable in the vortex of rapid change due to globalization, digitalization and the era of social media. Overall religion remain the source of peace making social cultural aspect of human civilization towards survive, sustain and harmony.

References

Behara, M.C. 2000. Tribal Religion: Change and Continuity. Commonwealth: New Delhi

Bhui, S and P, Mandal 2016 Significance of traditional community Festivals of the Santal in maintenance of Ecological Balance to reduce effect of Global Warming;pp-305-313 in Globalization: the missing Roads of the Tribal, Kalpaz, VP Sharma et al., Kalpaz, New Delhi

Dey, A 2015 An Ancient History: Ethnographic Study of the Santhal, International Journal of Novel Research in Humanity and Social Sciences Vol. 2, Issue 4, pp: (31-38), Month: July - August 2015,

H, A,Nikkhah. M,Zhairi.S, Sadeghi. M,Fani. 2015. The Mean Difference of Religiosity between Residents of Rural Areas and Urban Areas of Mahmoudabad City. Asian Social Science. Canadian Center of Science and

Education.11(2)

Hembrom, T. (1996). "The Santals", Published by Punthi&Pustak Publishers, Calcutta

Horton, R. (1960). A definition of religion, and its uses. The journal of the royal anthropological institute of Great Britain and Ireland, 90(2), 201-226.

Jana, K.S. (2008)Christianity and Tribal Identity: The Case of Santals of Bhimpore, West Bengal, *Man And Life* vol. 27 nos. 3-4 July-Dec.

Majumdar, D. N. (1995) The Santal- study in culture change, Manegerog Publication, Delhi.

Mandelbaum, D. G. (1966). Transcendental and Pragmatic Aspects of Religion 1. American Anthropologist, 68(5), 1174-1191.

Mandi, K.(2008) Santal Pujo Parbon (in Bengali), Bandowan, Purulia.

Panjabi, K 2010 "Otiter Jed" or Times of Revolution: Ila Mitra, the Santals and Tebhaga movement, *Economic and Political Weekly,* Vol. 45, No. 33 (AUGUST 14-20, 2010), pp. 53-59

Radcliff-Brown A R (1958) Methods in Social Anthropology , The University of Chicago Press, Illinois, USA

Raj, Selve J. & Dempsey, Corinne, (2000). "Popular Christianity in India", State University of New York Press, Albany

Saha, S. Goswami, N.(2019) Religious Life And Belief System Of The Santals-A Case Study In Solageria Village, *Man in India.* Serials Publications 93 (2-3) : 313 -332

Tudu, B.(2020) Saotal-Mohan PoromporarOnusondhaneByasto Ek Mohan JatirKotha. *Ananda Prokashon.* Kolkata.

Troiji, J. 1978. Tribal Religion; New Delhi : Manohar Publications.

Website

https://censusindia.gov.in/2011-Common/CensusData2011.html

https://www.indianmirror.com/tribes/santaltribes.html

https://www.lawctopus.com/academike/religious-conversion/

https://askanydifference.com/difference-between-catholic-and-protestant/

https://egyankosh.ac.in/bitstream/123456789/18895/1/Unit-27.pdf

Relationship among plant diversity, culture, and worship in sacred groves at Ajodhya Gram Panchayat, Purulia, W.B., India

Rajnarayan Podder: Research Scholar, Dept. of Anthropology and Tribal Studies, S. k. B University, Purulia, West Bengal, email-rajnarayanpodder92@gmail.com.

Dr. Sudip Bhui: Assistant professor, Dept. of Anthropology and Tribal Studies, S k B University, Purulia, West Bengal, email-bhuisudip@gmail.com

Abstract:

A forest is a sacred grove when it is worshipped and maintained by tribes and other castes. Different cultural features exist here. Varieties of different plants can be seen in this sacred grove. Data has been collected by questionnaire. The structured interview has conducted during the survey. Sacred groves GPS points have been taken by Garmin GPS. Sacred groves have been found in 15 out of 32 Mouza at Ajodhya Gram Panchayat in Purulia district. To find out if there is any relationship between the diversity of plants, culture, and worship in the sacred grove.

Key word: sacred grove, plant diversity, culture, worship.

Introduction:

The sacred grove is the natural virgin forest (Ormsby, A., 2013) or sacred forest where tribes and other communities worship their revered deities. It is a natural site (Mohanty, S., et al 2016) where a variety of flora and fauna can be observed. Secretary groups can be observed in different parts of the world as well as India. There are over 100000 sacred groups in different parts of India (Malhotra, K.C., et al, 2007). Large sacred groves are usually seen in the Himalayan region of Western Ghat North East India etc. (Singh, H., et al 2013; Kulkarni, A., et al 2018; Nganso, B. T., et al 2012). Cultural and spiritual relations can be observed in the sacred groves (Ormsby, A., 2013). Different types of cultural practices, rules, rituals, festivals, prohibitions, etc. are observed in the sacred groves (Hemrom, A. and Yadav, K.C., 2015; Mohanty, S., et al 2016). At present, due to the reduction, it's size, and biodiversity of the sacred groves, it is called remnant forest (Manna, S., et al 2017) and fragmented forest (Alohou, E. C., et al 2017). Worship has been practiced in the sacred groves for many ages, so there is a mythological and theological approach (Malik, V., 2015). Local attitude is one of the most effective attributes of this holy place (Ormsby, A., 2013). The management of the sacred grove is one of the important parts because this sacred place has been carrying its own identity for many years through traditional management (Vipat, A. and Bharucha, E., 2014). A sacred grove is a place of worship for various communities and they protect it in various ways. That is why different types of plants and animals are saved, that is, biodiversity has been preserved from the past (Singh, H., et al 2013; Prasad, M. R., et al 2015). Many old trees, endangered plants, and animals can be seen in this place. There are various medicinal plants in this place that are used to cure various human diseases (Bisoi, S. S., and Panda, D. 2015; Dey, A and Nath De, J., 2010).

Biodiversity was coined by Walter G. Rosenin in 1986. Biodiversity is one of the most useful and purposeful words for the modern world. It means the variety of flora and fauna of a place (Singh, S., et al 2017; Rawat U.S. and Agarwal N.K., 2015). Biodiversity can be divided into genetic diversity, species diversity, and ecosystem diversity (Rawat U.S. and Agarwal N.K., 2015, Pullaiah, T., et al 2015). Biodiversity is dependent on climate and the impact of climate change on biodiversity (Rathore, A. and Jasrai, Y.T., 2013). Different types of plants can be observed in different parts of the world which are called plant diversity (Pullaiah, T., et al 2015). Plant diversity is dependent on abiotic factors (Merganic, J., et al 2012). The plant continues to feed the animal kingdom in various ways and maintain the balance of the earth's ecosystems (Corlett, R.T., 2016; Merganic,J., et al 2012). Plant diversity is conserved by in situ and ex situ methods (Corlett, R.T., 2016). The variety of trees in the sacred grove can be noticed extensively.

culture refers to a combination of the languages, manners, characters, rules, norms, eating habits, dress, etc. of a particular group in a particular place which has been going on since ancient times (Lebrón, A.,2013; Brown,N., et al 2020). There are different types of cultural people living in different parts of the world and one cultural person is different from other cultural people. There has been a close relationship between man and nature since ancient times (Sambyal, R.S., 2017). The relationship between human culture and the environment is different in different parts of the world and this relationship is called cultural ecology (Lapka, M., et al 2012).

There are various kinds of work that have been done regarding the sacred grove. As ground-dwelling insect species have diversity in the Purulia district. Fragmentation effect on forest ecosystem and relation with forest reserve (Alohou, E. C., et al 2017). Butterfly diversity is seen in Ghana (Nganso, B. T., et al 2012). Festivals, traditions, and ritual importance with sacred groves in Chhattisgarh (Hemrom, A. and Yadav, K.C., 2015).Ecosystem conservation, Eczema medical analysis in the sacred grove at Koraput district (Bisoi, S. S., and Panda, D., 2015).Water conservation in the sacred groves (Mahajan, M., 2017). There is an Impact on the environment of sacred groves (Mahajan, M.,2018).In-situ biodiversity conservation in the rainforest zone (Onyekwelu, J. C., & Olusola, J. A., 2014). Sacred groves have Concepts, threats, and conservation of biodiversity (Rawat U.S. and Agarwal N.K., 2015). Climate change impacts biodiversity and importance (Rathore, A., 2013).

Objectives:

Small and big sacred groves can be seen in different places in the Purulia district. The features of the sacred groves of Ajodhya Gram Panchayat of Purulia district are significant. As the Gram Panchayat is located in the hills, most of the land is covered by forest and most of the forest belongs to the forest department. Here is a collection of different types of trees and animals. The tribes here have different cultural features. Main objective of the study are:

1) To find out big plant diversity of Ajodhya GP sacred groves
2) To find out the cultural characteristics of the Ajodhya gram panchayat

3) To find out the relationship between plant diversity, culture and worshiping in sacred groves

Study area:

The only plateau district in West Bengal is Purulia which is located in the west of the state. Its latitude and longitude are 22°42'35"N to 23°42'N and85°49'25"E to 86°54'37"E. There are 20 blocks in the Purulia district. Ajodhya Gram Panchayat (23°10'30"N to 23°16'30"N and86°1'30"E to 86°12'0"E) is part of the Baghmundi block and the main tourist spot of Purulia is Ajodhya Hill. The total area of Ajodhya GP is 1562.09 hectares, population of 1648 according to the 2011 census. There are 32 Mouza in Ajodhya Gram Panchayat and 15 sacred groves have been surveyed (table-1). According to the 2011 census about 75% of the scheduled tribes' population is here.

SI no	Name of sacred grove	Extension	Area in acress of sacred grove	No. of trees in sacred groves
	Table no- 1 surveyed area location, area and no. of trees			

SI no	Name of sacred grove	Extension	Area in acress of sacred grove	No. of trees in sacred groves
1	SAHARJURI	23°15'33.20"N 86° 6'11.10"E	0.82	35
2	KALHA	23°13'47.50"N 86° 6'45.80"E	0.45	12
3	RANGA	23°13'34.00"N 86° 4'52.00"E	0.86	64
4	TALIA BHASA	23°14'28.20"N 86° 4'16.50"E	0.73	80
5	HESADI	23°15'42.90"N 86° 5'10.00"E	0.85	37
6	BHITPANI	23°14'27.10"N 86° 3'29.70"E	0.52	122
7	PUNIA SHASAN	23°12'1.00"N 86° 8'40.90"E	0.38	26
8	SHIMUL BERA	23°11'52.10"N 86° 9'40.10"E	1.1	40
9	KALIJHARNA	23°11'42.50"N 86°10'27.30"E	1.71	222
10	USHULDUNGRI	23°11'53.80"N 86°10'23.30"E	0.26	19
11	CHHATRAJARA	23°12'60.00"N 86°11'25.50"E	0.26	36
12	LAHADUNGRI	23°13'5.56"N 86° 9'7.89"E	2.29	117
13	JAMGHUTU	23°13'21.95"N 86° 6'36.43"E	0.87	82
14	BHUINGHORA	23°14'7.50"N 86° 5'10.00"E	0.66	28
15	KUSUMTIKARI	23°14'48.00"N 86° 4'5.30"E	0.50	96
Total area and trees			12.26	1016

Surveyed year 2018

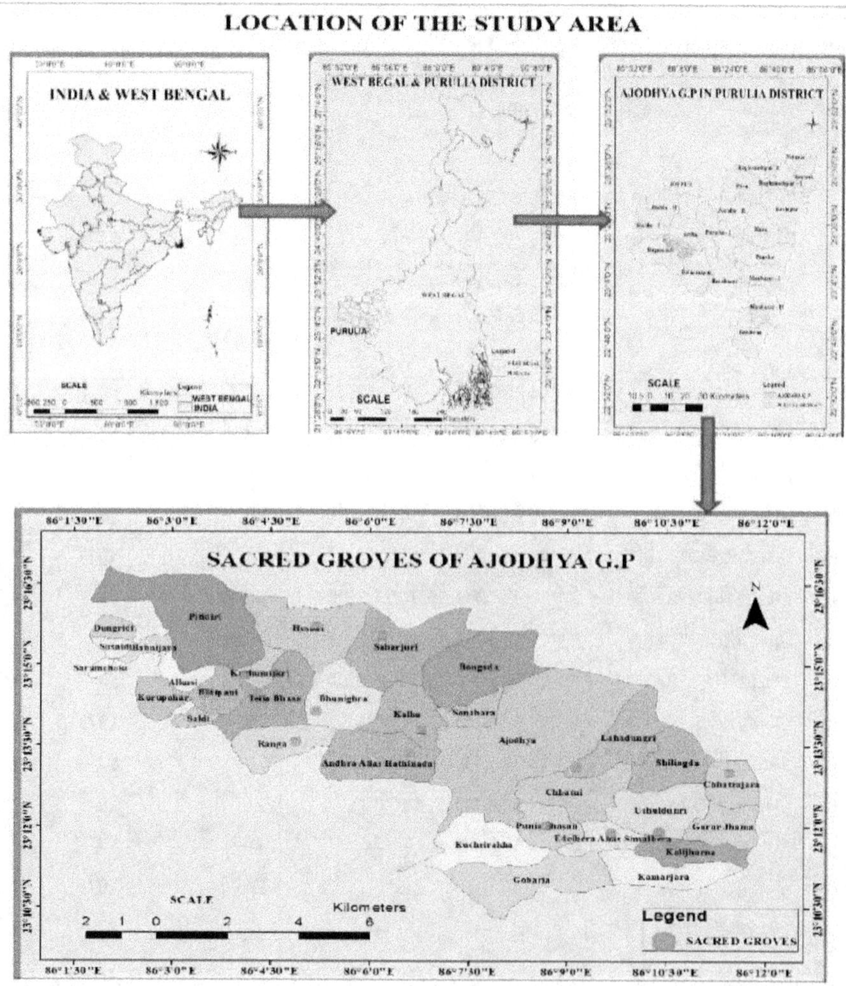

Methodology:

First, a pilot survey has been conducted in Ajodhya Gram Panchayat in January 2018. Then some information has been found about the sacred groves there in March 2018. A survey has been conducted to get information about the culture of the indigenous people along with a variety of plants in the sacred groves. To collect data a questionnaire has been created. Structured interview and personal interview has been conducted to know the cultural characteristics, and plant diversity. As the number of tribal is more in this gram Panchayat, their cultural influences can be noticed more in the sacred groves. 15 sacred groves have been surveyed out of 32 Mouza in the gram panchayat. Data have been taken for 30 minutes in each sacred grove. The information has been taken from old men and priests. GPS points have been taken from each grove. To do the study, most emphasis has been placed on primary data and less information has been used on secondary data. Both quantitative and qualitative data have been taken.

Result and discussion:

Plant diversity: Most of the forest lands of the Ajodhya Gram Panchayat fall under protected forest and belong to the forest range. Most of the sacred grove areas here belong to the forest department and some of the donor and collective places. Only large plants have been surveyed in this study. From table-2 it is understood that different types of plants have been observed here. During the survey, it has been noticed that there are many differences between the plants of the sacred groves and the plants of the surrounding area. The trees of the sacred groves are quite old and the trees around them are not old. A total of 44 types of trees have been found in the sacred groves of the Ajodhya Gram Panchayat and these trees fall into 24 families (table-2). Although there are many types of trees in Ajodhya, there are 44 types of trees in the sacred groves. The total area of 15 sacred groves is12.26 acres and the total number of trees is 1016 (table-1). The highest number of trees has been found at Kalijharna village about 222 (table-1).

Table no- 2 plants of Ajodhya G.P's Sacred groves.

Sl. No.	Scientific name of tree.	Family	Name of trees in Bengali term or local term.	No of the trees
1	Alangiumsalvifolium(Linn. f.) Wang	Alangiaceae	Akhura	3
2	BuchananialanzanSpreng	Anacardiaceae	Pial	40
3	Semecarpusanacardium Linn.f. Suppl		Bhella	30
4	MangiferaindicaLinn		Aam	1
5	Holarrhenaantidysenterica(Heyne ex Roth) A. DC.	Apocynaceae	Kurchi	13
6	Alstoniascholaris (L.) R. Br		ChhatimChhatim	10
7	Tabernaemontanacoronaria(Jacq.) Willd.		Tagar	2
8	Phoenix sylvestris(Linn.) Roxb	Arecaceae	Khejur	2
9	BorassusflabelliferLinn		Tal	2
10	Bombaxceiba.	Bombacaceae	Simul	2
11	TerminaliaaalataHeyne ex roth. Syn. T. tomentosa W.& A.	Combretaceae	Asan	102
12	Anogeissuslatifolia(DC.) Wall. Ex Bedd.		Dhaw	66
13	Terminaliachebula Retz.		Hartaki	4
14	Terminaliabellirica (Gaertn.)Roxb		Bahara	3
15	Terminaliaarjuna (Roxb.) Wight. Am		Arjun	1
16	Alangiumsalviifolium	cornaceae	Dhela	60
17	ShorearobustaGaertn.F.	Dipterocarpaceae Local	Sal	435
18	DiospyrosMelanoxylonRoxb.	Ebenaceae	Kend	57
19	Cleistanthuscollinus(Roxb.) Benth	Euphorbiaceae	Parasi	2
20	Acacia auriculiformis A. Cunn. exBenth.	Fabaceae	Akashmani /Sonajhuri	10
21	Vachellianilotica		babul	5
22	Tamarindusindica		Tetul	2
23	Delonixregia		Krishnacura	1
24	Lagerstroemia parvifloraRoxb	Lythraceae	Sidha	51
25	Azadirachtaindica A. Juss	Meliaceae	Nim	5
26	Albizialebbeck(Linn.) Benth.	Minosaceae	Siris	2

27	Ficusbenghalensis Linn.	Moraceae	Bot	4
28	FicusreligiosaLinn		Aswatha	2
29	Ficusvirens		Pakar	1
30	FicushispidaRoxb		Dumur	1
31	Eugenia jambolanaLamk.	Myrtaceae	Jam	3
32	Nyctanthesarbortristis	Oleaceae	Shiuli	2
33	Buteamonosperma(Lamk.) Taub	Papilionaceae	Palash	15
34	DalbergiasissooRoxb		Sisoo	1
35	PterocarpusmarsupiumRoxb.		Murga	1
36	ZizyphusmauritianaLamk	Rhamnaceae	Kul	6
37	Adina cordifolia(Roxb.) Hook. f. ex Brandis,	Rubiaceae	Karam	19
38	IxoraarboreaRoxb. ex Smith		Lohajangi	2
39	AnthocephaluscadambaMiq.		Kadam	2
40	Glycosmispentaphyllaauct. pl	Rutaceae	Sheora	1
41	Aeglemarmelos Corr.		Bel	1
42	Schleicheraoleosa (Lour.) Oken	Sapindaceae	Kusum	17
43	Madhucaindica J.F. Gmel	sapotaceae	mahul	17
44	TectonagrandisLinn.f	Verbenaceae	Segun	10
Surveyed year 2018				1016

Most seen plants are

Table 3 and pic-2 show that the trees that are most abundant here are Sal, Asan, Dhaw, Dhela, Kend, Sidha, Pial, Bhella, Karam, Kusum and the rest are very few. Of the 44 species of trees, most are Sal. Out of 1016 trees, 435 are Sal trees and most of the Sal trees are quite old and thick.

Table-3

sl no	tree name	no. of tree
1	Sal	435
2	Asan	102
3	Dhaw	66
4	dhela	60
5	Kend	57
6	Sidha	51
7	Pial	40
8	Bhella	30
9	Karam	19
10	Kusum	17
11	Others	139
	total	1016

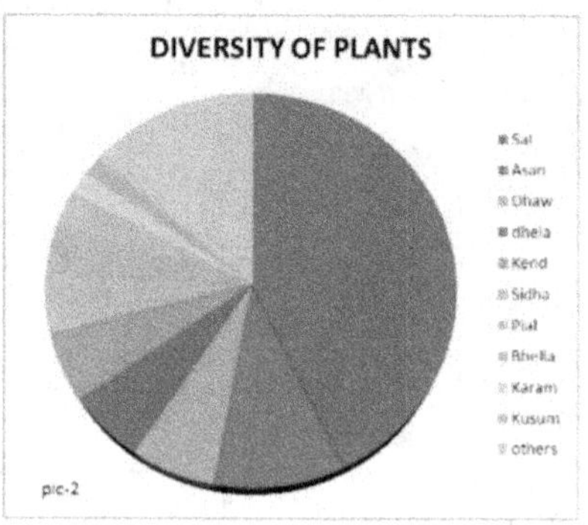

Plant Family diversity

From table-4 and pic-3 it is understood that 24 family trees are present here in the sacred groves. Of the 24 families, the Combretaceae family has the largest number of trees and then Ebenaceae, Moraceae, and Anacardiaceae, family respectively, other family trees are few like Myrtaceae, Oleaceae, Rhamnaceaeetc.

table-4

family of plant	no. of tree's type
Combretaceae	5
Fabaceae	4
Moraceae	4
Anacardiaceae	3
Apocynaceae	3
Papilionaceae	3
Rubiaceae	3
Arecaceae	2
Rutaceae	2
others family	15

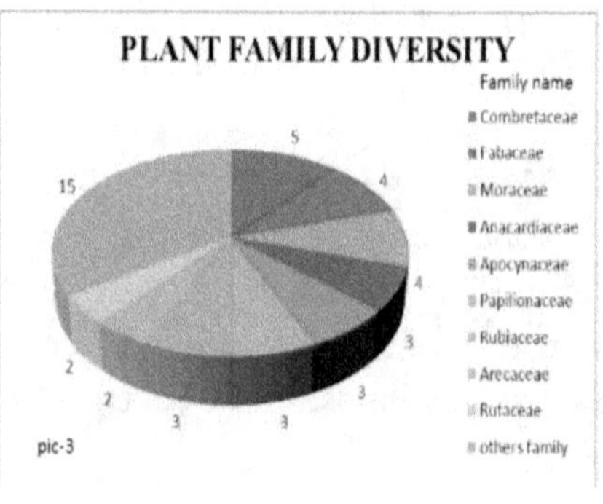

Culture: Differences between different groups can be noticed through culture, mainly through language, behavior, habit, norms, etc. Ajodhya Gram Panchayat is mostly inhabited by tribes and the tribal groups are Santal, Munda, Bhumij, etc. They speak the Santali language among themselves and use the Alchiki script. Apart from the Santal language, they can speak Bengali and Hindi. These indigenous people enjoy different festivals at different times of the Year like Sarhul/ Baha, Saharai, Karam,

Maghi, etc. The hunting festival is celebrated on the day of Buddha Purnima. On the day of Buddha Purnima, gatherings are held in the sacred groves of Gordham, and hunting festivals are celebrated throughout the day. The main folk dance of the Purulia district is the Chhau dance and many tribal of this Gram Panchayat are associated with this dance. During Puja, men wear dhoti and ganji and women wear red and white sarees.

Sacred groves and worshiping: There are sacred groves almost everywhere in the 32 Mouza of Ajodhya Gram Panchayat. 15 sacred groves have been found in 32 Mouza and information has been gathered from there. The sacred grove is called "Jaher Than" by the tribal. The name of the deity worshipped here are Marangburu, JaherAya, Rangaburi, Lukapath, etc. They worship the trees as a symbol of God such as Sal, Kusum, etc. Worship is done at certain times of the Year and some people worship every day. An altar with four sticks is built under the Sal, Kusum etc. tree and worship is done. Only the Shahrul or Baha festival is celebrated in the Jaher Than. The Baha festival is celebrated for three days after the full moon in March. The word Baha means "festival of flowers". The 3 days program is called Um, Sardi, and Jale respectively. After the puja, the girls dance in groups.

Conclusion:

The tribes see nature as a God and usually address the tree as their God. There are different types of plants in the sacred groves of Ajodhya Gram Panchayat and the plants are very old. The study suggests that this place is full of plant diversity. Various cultural events are held here by the Baha festival in the sacred grove. They worship under the Sal tree and dance and sing in groups at this place. One of their cultural festivals is the Baha's festival and which is celebrated in the sacred grove, where they worship the Sal tree and other trees as deities. So, different types of trees have been preserved for many years through their cultural worship. From this, it is understood that a close relationship has developed the diversity of plants, culture, and worship in the sacred groves.

References:

Alohou, E. C., Gbemavo, D. S. J. C., Mensah, S. and Ouinsavi, C. (2017), 'Fragmentation of Forest Ecosystems and Connectivity Between Sacred Groves and Forest Reserves in Southeastern Benin',West Africa, Tropical Conservation Science, 10, 1–11.

Behera, J. and Samal, R. M. (2015), 'Category (Tribe and Non-Tribe) As a Factor in Educational Aspiration of Secondary School Students: An Investigation', IOSR Journal of Research & Method in Education (IOSR-

JRME),5(4), 01-11.

Bisoi, S. S., and Panda, D. (2014), 'Ethno-medicinal plants present in sacred groves of koraput district of odisha', India, ActaBiomedicaScientia, 2(1), 39-42.

Brown,N., McIlwraith, T., and González L.T.(2020),'Perspectives: an open introduction to cultural anthropology' Second edition, Arlington, American Anthropological Association.

Corlett, R.T. (2016), 'Plant diversity in a changing world: Status, trends, and conservation needs', Plant Diversity, 38, 10-16.

Dey, A and Nath De, J. (2010), 'A Survey of Ethnomedicinal Plants used by the tribals of Ajoydha Hill Region, Purulia District, India', American-Eurasian Journal of Sustainable Agriculture, 4(3), 280-290.

Hemrom, A. and Yadav, K.C. (2015), 'Festivals, traditions & rituals associated with sacred groves of Chhattisgarh', International Journal of Multidisciplinary Research and Development, 2(2), 15-21.

Kulkarni, A., Upadhye, A., Dahanukar, N., & Datar, M. N. (2018). Floristic uniqueness and effect of degradation on diversity: A case study of sacred groves from northern Western Ghats. *Tropical Ecology*, *59*(1), 119-127.

Kumar, A., Fuloria, K. and Taunk, A. (2012), '), A comparative study of tribal and non-tribal women in the state of Uttarakhand (India) in the field of women's autonomy', contraceptive used and family planning, Journal of Research in Peace, Gender and Development, 2(7), 156-161.

Lapka, M., Vávra, B., and Sokolíčková, Z. (2012), 'Cultural ecology: contemporary understanding of the relationship between humans and the environment', Journal of Landscape Ecology, 5(2).

Lebrón, A., MBA, DBA, (2013), 'What is Culture?', Merit Research Journal of Education and Review, 1(6), 126-132.

Lone, M. M. and Khan, M. A. (2018), 'A Comparative Study of Social Intelligence of Tribal and Non-Tribal Students of Kashmir', International Journal of Creative Research Thoughts IJCRT, 6(1), 1522-1531.

Mahajan, M. and Patil, R. (2018), Impact of sacred groves on the environment, I J R B A T, VI (I), 5-6

Mahajan, M. ansfatima, S. (2017), 'water conservation in sacred groves', Epitome: International journal of Multidisciplinary reaches, 3(7), 17-21.

Malhotra, K.C., Gokhale, Y., Chatterjee, S., and Srivastava, S. (2007), 'Sacred groves in India', New Delhi, Aryan books international.

Malik, V. (2015), 'Addition to the sacred grove of India', Journal of Global Biosciences, 4(7), 2699-2702.

Mandal, R. P., Pati, S., Sarkar, S., Gayen, A., Guin, P. and Mishra, T. (2015), 'General awareness and perception about sacred groves and biodiversity conservation in urban people of Bankura district, West Bengal, India, Int. res. J. Environment Sci., 4(2), 16-21.

Manna, S., Manna, S., Ghora, T. and Roy, A. (2017), 'Sacred grove as remnant forest: A vegetation analysis', BIODIVERSITAS, 18 (3), 899-908.

Merganic,J., Merganičová, K., Marušák, R., and Audolenská, V. (2012), ' Plant Diversity of Forests', Forest Ecosystems,Croatia.

Mohanty, S., Das, P. K. and Kumar, S. (2016), 'Role of Sacred Groves in the Conservation of Traditional Values of Odisha', Advances in Plants & Agriculture Research, 3(3), 1-4.

Nganso, B. T., Kyerematen, R., & Obeng-Ofori, D. (2012). Diversity and abundance of butterfly species in the Abiriw and Odumante sacred groves in the Eastern Region of Ghana. *Research in Zoology*, 2(5), 38-46.

Onyekwelu, J. C., & Olusola, J. A. (2014). Role of sacred grove in in-situ biodiversity conservation in rainforest zone of south-western Nigeria. *Journal of Tropical Forest Science*, 5-15.

Ormsby, A. (2013), 'Analysis of local attitudes toward the sacred groves of Meghalaya and Karnataka, India' Conservation and Society, 11(2), 187-197.

Prasad, M. R., Subhadip, P., Soumik, S., Arpan, G., Priya, G., & Trisha, M. (2015). General awareness and Perceptions about Sacred Groves and Biodiversity Conservation in Urban people of Bankura District, West Bengal, India. *Int. Res. J. Environment Sci*, 4(2), 16-21

Pullaiah, T., Bahadur, B., and Krishnamurthy, K. V. (2015), 'Plant Biodiversity', Plant Biology and Biotechnology, 1.

Purkayastha, N. (2016), 'Concept of indian tribes: an overview', International Journal of Advanced Research in Management and Social Sciences, 5(3), 1-9.

Rathore, A. and Jasrai, Y.T. (2013), 'Biodiversity: Importance and Climate Change Impacts', International Journal of Scientific and Research Publications, 3(3).

Rawat U.S. and Agarwal N.K (2015), 'Biodiversity: Concept, threats and conservation', Environment Conservation Journal, 16(3), 19-28.

Sambyal, R.S. (2017), 'Sacred Groves and Ancient Principles of Conservation', Imperial Journal of Interdisciplinary Research (IJIR), 3(6),

120-124.

Singh, H., Agnihotri, P., Pande, P.C. and Husain, T. (2013), 'Role of Traditional Knowledge in Conserving Biodiversity: A Case Study from PatalBhuvneshwar Sacred Grove, Kumaon Himalaya, India', Journal of Biodiversity Management & Forestry, 2(2), 1-5.

Singh, S., Youssouf, M., Malik, Z. A., & Bussmann, R. W. (2017). Sacred groves: myths, beliefs, and biodiversity conservation—a case study from Western Himalaya, India. *International journal of ecology, 2017.*

Sonpimple, R. P. (2012), 'Conceptualizing tribes from differnt disciplinary and ideological perspectives', EXCEL International Journal of Multidisciplinary Management Studies, 2(3), 107-116.

Vipat, A. and Bharucha, E., (2014), 'Sacred Groves: The Consequence of Traditional Management', Journal of Anthropology, 1-8.

CHAPTER NINE

Role of traditional agricultural knowledge practice of Santal tribal people of Purulia district, W.B, India

Rajnarayan Podder: Research Scholar, Dept. of Anthropology and Tribal Studies, S. k. B. University, Purulia, West Bengal, email-rajnarayanpodder92@gmail.com.

Anima Besra: Student of Dept. of Anthropology and Tribal Studies, 3rd sem., S. k. B. University, Purulia, West Bengal, email-animabesra653@gmail.com

Dr.Sudip Bhui: Assistant professor, Dept. of Anthropology and Tribal Studies, S. k. B. University, Purulia, West Bengal, email-bhuisudip@gmail.com

Abstract:

GDP from the agricultural sector is 20.19% in 2020-21. Agriculture is one of the livelihood and income sources of the Santal community of West Bengal, Jharkhand, Orissa, Bihar, and Assam. The Santals cultivate crops according to their own rules, which have been passed down through generations called traditional knowledge. This study has been done to see whether the Santals are still farming based on traditional agricultural knowledge, or farming according to modern practices. It has also been seen that the crops that were cultivated 50 years ago are still grown. For this study, primary data have been collected in Lukuidi village of BamundiMouza in Puncha block of Purulia district. Both qualitative and quantitative methods have been used and data has been collected from 86 respondents. The crops cultivated 50 years ago as Mawra, Kadwa, Bajra, Wheat, etc. are not grown now, but the Santals are still cultivating crops based on traditional knowledge.

Key words: Traditional knowledge, agriculture, Santal people, crops,

Introduction:

Agriculture is the backbone of the Indian economy and most of the Indian population depends on it, basically rural people (Syiem, R., & Raj, S., 2015). Indigenous Technology Knowledge (ITK) is the treasure of the tribal population of India which leads to the management of local natural resources with the help of various techniques of indigenous people (Shakrawar, M., &Naberia, S., 2018). Physical, natural, financial, human, and social capitals are five core human activity assets that built the livelihood of humans. The livelihood of tribal people depends on natural resources and traditional agricultural activity. Paddy cultivation is predominant among the Santals, providing them with food throughout the year. Poverty alleviation policies improve tribal people's sustainable agriculture for good livelihood (Patidar, J. et al., 2018). Traditional agricultural knowledge is differing from scientific agricultural studies and tribal people maintain unwritten traditional agricultural knowledge from ancient times with practice, which is the backbone of the economy of Valat at Wayanad (Shilja, K. V., &Hasees, P., 2018). Langala (wooden country plough), Bida(harrow), Bahangi (caring rod made of an elastic piece of wood or bamboo), Buria (small axe), Sabal (iron rod), Da (sickle), etc. are tribal agricultural equipment of Bamanghati sub-division in Mayurbhanj district of Orissa and this cultivation equipment have been changed due to modernization. There is a relationship between agriculture and social festival worship in the tribal community, as at the time of sowing seed 'Erok' worship, crop growing time 'SuraSasanMalmane', worship to Jahere era with new crop at 'JomNowa' etc. (Mahapatra, S., 1978).

Tribal people live in forests, and hill regions with their dialect, and primitive religion. Tribal people's occupation is hunting, gleaning, gathering, etc. another side they created their social common government, and totemism, animism, and nature worship are part of the tribal community (Purkayastha, N., 2016). There are harmonious tribal social systems and agriculture production techniques with nature. Tribal agricultural activity transformed from shifting to a settled agricultural economy (Morey, S. D. et al, 2010). Climate condition is important for agricultural activity. Department of Interior Climate Science Centre (CSCs),

Landscape Conservation Cooperatives and Bureau of Indian Affairs (BIA), etc. Federal climate coordination networks help tribes to build resource capacity with agriculture production in the USA (Reyes, J. J, et al, 2018). Organic agriculture is part of tribal people's practice for a long time but they also practice shifting cultivation at present as Naga tribal people of North-East of India. International Federation of Organic Agricultural Movement (IFOAM) is an organic organization that helps farmers to plant organic agricultural systems with healthy ecology (Eernstman, N., &Wals, A. E. J., 2009). ChuktiaBhunjia tribal people of central India as Maharashtra, Chhatishgah, and Orissa, practiced shifting cultivation for a long time but at present, they practiced paddy cultivation with their traditional knowledge and short-duration paddies are Lachei, Kalikhuji, Jhuli, etc. (Sabar, B.). Forestry, shifting cultivation, settled agriculture, fishing, etc. are the economic activity of Kerala's 35 tribal people as Paniya, Adiya, Kattunaikan, Korayas, Kadar, etc. They depend on natural resources for agricultural production and the adult tribal people of Kerala have a lot of knowledge regarding traditional agriculture (KB, N., 2010). ICT plays a very important role in the 'global information age' and it can improve rural people's agricultural knowledge. Television show regarding agriculture is good for rural people as Kissan TV channel of Doordarshan Kendra Shillong (Meghalaya) helps local people as well as rural tribal people. ICT helps livestock management, rural health, rural education, commercial service, etc. (Syiem, R., & Raj, S.).

Indigenous or tribal knowledge study is the new research area of Anthropology to identify their primitive practice for development (Pramukh, K. R., &Palkumar, P. D. S., 2006). Santal people are calm men according to Santal word and one of the dominant tribal populations of N.E India as West Bengal, Jharkhand, Orissa, Bihar, and Assam. Farming, fishing, hunting, and forest resource collecting are the livelihood activity of the Santal people but the cultivation of various crops are present occupation (Tudu, M., & Das, S. K., 2022). Rice is taken as the main food of the Santal people and Jadhan, Bahiyad and Bad were rice varieties of traditional cultivation of Jharkhand. Indigenous food habits have rich sources of micronutrients which they get from the forest, own cultivation, etc. food (Ghosh-Jerath, S. et al, 2016).

Objectives:

Traditional knowledge is a powerful weapon of the tribal community for their life. The main objectives of this study are

1_ To find out the traditional knowledge of tribal people regarding agricultural activity

2_ To find out Santal people's agricultural activity as present and past

3_ To find out the change in the agricultural practice of Santal people's primitive knowledge

Methodology:

Study area:

Lukuiditola or village of Bamundimouza in Puncha block of Purulia district is located on the north-south edge, inhabited by the Santal community. The Santal community has a large population in this village and is an old village, besides being quite far from Purulia town. Various tribes of Santals live within this village, including the Murmu, Mandi, Hembram, Besra, Tudu, Hansda, and Saran. The village is surrounded by forests, from which the native Santals of the village bring fuel wood and dry leaves. The current population data of the village obtained from an ICDS worker is 336 out of which males 172 and females 164.

Methods:

For this study, a survey was conducted in September 2022 at Lukuidi village of Puncha block in the Purulia district. The village was selected for the high percentage of the Santal tribal population and most of the people engaged in agricultural activity with tribal knowledge according to the pilot survey. They live in other communities also. For this study, primary and secondary data have been collected with mixed methodology. Quantitative and qualitative data were used to know the tribal agricultural knowledge of the Santal people of Lukuidi village. This study is based on descriptive research because the Santal people's agricultural knowledge does have not enough data. Qualitative data is used more than quantitative data to know their experience of agricultural activity with their knowledge. Other side data is also collected from secondary source as a journal, papers, books, etc.

The total Santal population of the village is 336 out of these 86 were selected randomly to collect data. Data was divided into three stratified categories below 30, 30-50, and above 50 years, and data was collected male/ female randomly. For data collection, a structured schedule had created for data collection of agricultural activity. Group interviews and personal interviews have been done during data collection. After data collection, data have been analysed. Weightage factor analysis has been used to know traditional knowledge apply in cultivation (Terang, P. P. et al, 2015). Weightage distribution as 1 (modern technology apply), 2 (traditional knowledge & modern technology apply), and 3(traditional knowledge apply) (table-1).

Table no. – 1 Weightage index		
Serial No.	Factor	weightage
1	Modern technology apply	1
2	traditional knowledge & modern technology apply	2
3	traditional knowledge apply	3

Result and discussion:

For this study, the survey was conducted in September, during the paddy growing season. As all had engaged in farming during the survey, respondents have been identified by random sampling and data have been collected into three categories. As the middle-aged population is more prominent, more information is available to them. Qualitative information about traditional farming has obtained from 86 respondents (table-2).

Table No. -2 data collection from Lukuidi village				
Age group	Male	Female	Total no of sample	Percentage (%)
Below 30	18	8	26	30.23
30-50	21	16	37	43.02
Above 50	13	10	23	26.75
Total	52	34	86	100%
Source: survey in Sep. 2022				

Are the crops that were cultivated about 50 years ago still being cultivated? In answer to this question, 95 percent of the respondents said that crops had been cultivated earlier, but those crops are not cultivated now. They used to cultivate crops such as Mawra, Kadwa, Bajra, Wheat, Paddy, etc. to satisfy their family's hunger. These crops had cultivated in open fields and cultivated at fixed times to spend their daily lives. These crops are not cultivated now, but even if they are cultivated, they are cultivated to maintain the old tradition. Cultivation is not done to satisfy hunger as it used to be. Some of the crops that were grown earlier are described.

A) Kadwa- after fertilizing the land with a plow, the seeds were spread and covered with soil. This crop is not cultivated now.

B) Paddy- the rice that was cultivated earlier was different from the rice of today. That rice was grown in open fields and required little water. The land of Purulia is ups and downs, based on cultivation four types of land are known here as Bahal, Kanali, Baid, and Tard. At that time, most of the farming was done on Bahal and Kanali land. At that time, people cultivated the land with hand-drawn plows.

C) Millet- the millet crop was cultivated on the vacant land next to the house. The soil was plowed with hand-drawn plough, da, sabal, etc. and then dung was sprinkled to fertilize the land. Then millet crop was cultivated but now this crop is not cultivated.

D) Wheat- wheat was cultivated then but now wheat is not cultivated.

Over time, some changes in farming practices have taken place, other crops are now being cultivated instead of the crops that were originally cultivated. The crops that were grown earlier were very low yielding and not satisfactory. Although the cultivation of crops has changed, the method of cultivating them has remained almost the same. Earlier crops were grown on vacant land but now crops are grown on cultivable land. Various new types of seeds, especially rice, have brought many changes and production is also increasing. Decades ago, the seeds of the crop were allowed to ripen well and the seeds were stored for next year's cultivation. But at present, the crops are cultivated by buying marketed seeds.

What crops do you currently cultivate and how do you do it? Although different people give different opinions on this question, they cultivate according to their old customs. At present, the Santal people of Lukuidi village mainly cultivate paddy and various vegetables during the rest of the year. Table three gives some information about cultivation methods. In addition to their traditional farming methods, it is also seen whether they are using modern technology. Among the information obtained from 86 respondents, most of the Santal people of the village are farming according to their traditional rules.

Table No.-3 Trace out application of traditional knowledge among various age group of Santal people of Lukuidi village						
Age group	Modern technology apply		Traditional knowledge and modern technology		Traditional Knowledge apply	
	frequency	weightage	frequency	Weightage	frequency	weightage
Below 30	7	1	14	2	5	3
30-50	8	1	16	2	13	3
Above 50	0	1	7	2	16	3
Total weightage	15		74		102	
Weightage calculation: first, frequency × weightage, then add all groups in particular factor						

Using modern technology is weightage 15, using both traditional knowledge and modern technology is weightage 74, and farming based on traditional technology alone is weightage 102 (table-3). This shows that despite the modern touches, they continue to rely on their traditions and continue farming. Currently, people under 30 years of age want to use modern technology, but they are unable to use things in that way. Because according to them farming in their method only meets their needs but cannot sell the crops. For financial reasons, some cannot use modern equipment, they would have been able to produce more crops and sell them in the market, according to them. However, people above fifty are willing to continue according to their traditions, rules, and methods.

Traditional way cultivation

The Santals currently cultivate the land with cow-drawn plough and use bio-fertilizers for better farming, according to them. But those who are financially better off plow the land with the help of tractors. Before planting paddy and any other crops, they perform various kinds of worship, which they believe will bring a good harvest. Still, villagers make manure from cow dung and rotting vegetables and use it as organic fertilizer for agriculture. Plow, spade, crowbar, hoe, etc. are used for cultivation. The worship that is done with cultivation is discussed.

Rohini festival- Rohini festival is specially celebrated in Jaishtha (may-June) month i.e. summer season (Situng in the Santal language) and for paddy cultivation. The main purpose of doing this is to pray for a good harvest. Every farmer prays to god for a good harvest. On this day puja is performed in the cultivation field, mainly soil worship, so that the seedlings grow well and there is no disturbance in the cultivation in the future. Both women and men fast on the day of Rohini Puja. Some seeds are sown on this day by cutting the soil in the cultivated land. After worshiping the land, the soil is brought home and spread around the house and also placed in rice balls. On this day puja is performed at God's place under the holy tree of the village and various animals are sacrificed there.

Dasai/ Dansha festival- This festival is celebrated by Santals in the month of Ashwin (September-October).this festival is nature-oriented and for agriculture and on the other hand, this festival is for exploring the heritage. In this festival worship is performed beside the cultivated land and branches of trees called 'Dali' are planted in paddy fields. Atap rice or Sunned rice powder is spread in the fields and a 'Dali' is also planted where the dung is left to dry. This puja or worship is mainly done for rain so that there is no problem with farming.

Sohrai festival- Sohrai festival is one of the festivals with close association with agriculture. The festival takes place in the month of Kartik (October –November) according to village timings. The Sohrai festival is specially done for cows and buffaloes because it is a festival to respect cows and buffaloes. The Santals cultivate the land with cows, and buffaloes and their labour produces good crops. This is why this festival is celebrated. Before this festival, every house in the village is decorated anew. The walls of the house are coated with mud. Pictures are drawn on it with different colours. Cows and buffaloes are worshiped and worshiped for four days.

Chhata festival- Chhata festival is an ancient festival of the Purulia district which has been celebrated for a long time. The Santals celebrated this festival for the rainfall that is required for farming. This festival is held in Bhadra month (17th September). In this festival, Sal trees (Shorearobusta) are brought in the morning and first placed in front of the door and then taken to the fields. However, this festival is celebrated by many villagers in certain places. After performing worship with an umbrella-shaped stick covered with white cloth, the Chhata is raised according to the order of the current dynasty. The Chhata festival is held in different places in the Purulia district. Among them, the ChakoltorChhata festival is held most splendidly. Many Lukuidi villagers participate in this Chhata festival to worship and perform various functions throughout the night with their relatives.

Makar festival- Makar festival is the festival of bringing home new crops and enjoying joy. This festival takes place on the last day of Paush month (January), which is called PaushSankranti. Different types of pithas (sweet) are made by pounding new slope rice.

At present, rice cultivation is more common in Lukuidi village. Also, the crops or vegetables that are grown are Pulses, Maize, Chickpea, Peas, Cucumber, Watermelon, Brinjal, Radish, Almonds, Cabbage, Cauliflower, Pumpkin, Potato, Shrimp, etc. These crops are cultivated according to their custom and traditional knowledge.

Conclusion:

From the above discussion, it is clear that the Santal community people of Lukuidi village are still cultivating different types of crops through their traditional knowledge. Traditional agricultural knowledge is the method and rules that have been cultivated for generations and are maintained by the current generation. Despite the advent of modern agricultural technology, they still perform the pujas for agriculture and cultivate with plows, oxen, cows, buffaloes, etc. The festivals of Rohini, Dasai, Chhata, Makar, etc. are associated with farming work. Every festival is done to worship nature so that it rains on time, the weather is good condition. There has been some change in farming in the hope of some modern touches among the people below 30 years, but overall the village is maintaining its traditional farming. 50 years ago crops such as Mawra, Kadwa, Bajra, Wheat, etc. had cultivated for the relief of hunger but these crops are not cultivated now instead rice cultivation is more prevalent. Along with paddy cultivation, various vegetables and fruits are cultivated. Now someone produces more crops and markets them. Through this study, the Santal community people are still maintaining the tradition of farming through old traditional knowledge.

References:

Eernstman, N., &Wals, A. E. J. (2009). Interfacing knowledge systems: introducing certified organic agriculture in a tribal society. NJAS: Wageningen Journal of Life Sciences, 56(4), 375-390.

Ghosh-Jerath, S., Singh, A., Magsumbol, M. S., Kamboj, P., & Goldberg, G. (2016).Exploring the potential of indigenous foods to address hidden hunger: nutritive value of indigenous foods of Santal tribal community of Jharkhand, India.Journal of hunger & environmental nutrition, 11(4), 548-568.

KB, N. (2010).Agriculture knowledge and perception in tribal communities, KB, N. (2010).Agriculture knowledge and perception in tribal communities, 9(3), 531-535.

Mahapatra, S. (1978). Modernisation of Tribal Agriculture: Technological and Cultural Constraints. Economic and Political Weekly, 581-585.

Morey, S. D., Tekale, V. S., &Bhagat, G. J. (2010).DETERMINANTS OF KNOWLEDGE AND ADOPTION OF AGRICULTURAL PRACTICES BY ANDH TRIBAL. Green Farming, 1(3), 311-313.

Patidar, J., Kumhar, B., Mhaske, S., &Jat, S. (2018).Importance of Sustainable Agriculture in Tribal Community of India. International Journal of Bio-resource and Stress Management, 9(2), 253-256.

Pramukh, K. R., &Palkumar, P. D. S. (2006). Indigenous knowledge: Implications in Tribal health and disease. Studies of Tribes and Tribals, 4(1), 1-6.

Purkayastha, N. (2016). Concept of Indian Tribes: An Overview. International Journal of Advanced Research in Management and Social Sciences, 5(2), 1-9.

Reyes, J. J., Wiener, J. D., Doan-Crider, D., & Novak, R. (2018). Building collaborative capacity: supporting tribal agriculture and natural resources in a changing climate. Renewable Agriculture and Food Systems, 33(3), 222-224.

Sabar, B. (2010). Tribal Agriculture: The ChuktiaBhunjias in Central India. Economic and Political Weekly, 77-79.

Shakrawar, M., &Naberia, S. (2018).Socio-economic characteristics of tribal farmers practicing indigenous technical knowledge in agriculture. Journal of Pharmacognosy and Phytochemistry, 7(4), 884-886.

Shilja, K. V., &Hasees, P. (2018), Scientific Study on Indigenous Tribal Knowledge: Factors Affect-ing the Germination of Paddy, CPUH-Research Journal, 3(2), 222-225.

Syiem, R., & Raj, S. (2015). Access and usage of ICTs for agriculture and rural development by the tribal farmers in Meghalaya state of North-East India. Agrarinformatika/Journal of Agricultural Informatics, 6(3), 24-41.

Terang, P. P., Bisoyi, S. K., &Chandna, V. K. (2015, October). Weightage factor analysis between Programme Outcomes and Course Outcomes: A case study. In 2015 IEEE 3rd International Conference on MOOCs, Innovation and Technology in Education (MITE) (pp. 84-87).IEEE.

Tudu, M., & Das, S. K. (2022). The Santal Community Socio-Economical Information needs and Quality of Life: A case study at Saragchhida Village under Chandua Block in Mayurbhanj District of Odisha. Journal of Positive School Psychology, 6895-6906.

https://statisticstimes.com/economy/country/india-gdp-sectorwise.php

Unearthing the Significance of the Nature in the life of the Tribals of Jharkhand-Symbolic Discussion

Pragya Jha: PhD Research Scholar, Presidency College, Chennai

Abstract

There is always a symbiotic relationship between the Adivasis and the nature. The unsaid and a platonic relationship of the nature and Adivasi is explored in this paper. Jacinta Kerketta, a young and outspoken poet defines the lines and the draws the picture of the struggles of the tribals of Jharkhand and she raises concern over the same with her work. She incorporates the symbol of nature which is an absolute necessity in the life of the tribals. The disrupted relationship which is on the verge of further degradation is evoked by her in her works. While elaborating that relationship, she makes sure of even highlighting their struggles, the oppressions they face and how they are exploited.

Introduction

> "Twinkle Twinkle little star,
> ......Like a diamond in the sky"

Nursery rhymes and childhood tales always consisted of nature as the main element, symbol, tool etc. There are questions about why was it important for a child to understand nature. Why is nature sometimes playing a prominent role? Why does a human kid need to understand nature? The reason fairly stated by many critics was to establish a relationship between man and nature from the initial stage of life. The story does not end there, it actually starts from there. As we grow up, we realise that even our religion talks about nature's importance. Our culture teaches us to have fair treatment towards nature. Sooner orlater, we recognise that nature becomes an imminent part of our life. We have always been in a symbiotic relationship with nature. Whether we learn about it socially, culturally, religiously or sometimes lawfully, to study more about this relationship, French writer, Francoise d' Eaubonne coined the term ecofeminism. Eco-feminism was believed to be a theory that harps onthe idea of the relationship of a female with nature. As the study further evolved, it talked about the relationship of human beings with nature.

In literature, we have used the symbol of nature in every era. Perhaps the only other truth ascribable to the role of nature in literature is that it has demonstrated near-constant fluidity, from the dawn of English literature to the contemporary era. Homer in his creation *Iliad* or Virgil in the *Aeneid*explained the grim scenes, the dark scenes and the dramatic scenes with the help of nature. In *Beowulf* too, the swamp represented power. Then comes Chaucer who wrote in *The Canterbury Tales*, "April with his shores sote, The droughts of March hath perced to the rote." The month of April has been glorified as providing newness in life. In John Milton's *Paradise Lost* we see the depiction of hell and heaven. The depiction portrays human morality, consciousness and vision. The two spaces project the character of humans in real life. During the Middle Ages- Renaissance and Restoration- nature played a backdrop role. Nature was treated as a paper on which the stories and the conflicts of humans take place. The most important role of nature came in the Romantic Period. The period where essentialism of nature was the theme of the literary works. Nature was celebrated and given the pedestal of purity. Nature was described as the friend, the partner, the soulmate, the caregiver, the guardian and the mentor. The different shades of nature were glorified. Nature was calm and composed on one hand, while on the other hand, the nature was presented in all its wilderness. It was mighty and powerful for human beings. Though nature was the only comfort space for the Romantics,in the Victorian era again, nature was in the backdrop. Science evolved and with that, the subject also changed. The technology and science can be seen on the front foot. Nature was still visible in works of literature. In *The Scarlet Letter*, Nathaniel Hawthorne used nature to show the change in the scenes. It also draws the border between the good people and the bad. Further, the use of nature became hollower in Modern times,though T.S. Eliot still used nature exquisitely. When he used

April as 'the cruellest month' he was referring to April as a second month of Spring which results in the sprouting of the unhappy memories. The nature has been continuously used to provide a setting for most Modern poems. Then there are post-modern writers who went back and instead of using nature as a canvas, sometimes used it as a subject. The post-modern writers sometimes even proudly declared the nature as the centre which was lost in the Modern era.

As the avid chronology shows, Nature has always been omnipresent for the tribals. The tribals of Jharkhand have considered nature as an imminent part of their cultural significance. Their festivals revolve around the season changes, the flowering, the tree is celebrated etc. For example, the festival of Sarhul is being celebrated by the tribals of Jharkhand marking the importance of the Spring season. Sarhul means worshipping the trees. This festival signifies the importance of nature in the lives of the tribal communities of Jharkhand. Nature is engraved in their folk songs, stories and even in their literature scripts. It is embossed in their literature, their religion, their society's rules, their food, their struggles, their pain and even in their relief. They have always worshipped nature and considered it their companion.

Nature in the eyes of a tribal is being depicted in much tribal literature. One of such work of literature is *Angor* by Jacinta Kerketta. Jacinta Kerketta is a poet, writer and journalist. She belongs to Oraon community of Jharkhand and has consistently watched the tribals closely. Her works are a beautiful depiction of the different voices of these people. She has worked in voicing the struggles of the tribal communities, uplifting the necessity of the equality deserved by these people and sometimes she has voiced the weak, feeble voices of the women in these communities. She feels an instant and close connection with nature. While reminiscing her childhood memories, she often discusses how the nature was an important part of her life. Nature is the subject, a symbol, an element, a tool etc. in the works of Kerketta. This work will unravel her journey of life with the help of nature in the book *Angor*.

Angor is a book which is relatable, yet a fierce portrayal of reality. It portrays an unsettling and grim truth faced by the Adivasis of Jharkhand. It is the journey of oppression, the inequality and the inferior treatment that further results in pain, anguish and suffering for the people. She has successfully portrayed everything in her work. Calling it just tribal literature will not do justice to the work she has produced. She has possibly enclosed the smell of the lands of Jharkhand in her work. She has depicted the rich culture and the beauty.

"O, city!
Leaving behind their homes,
Their soil, and bales of straw
Fleeing the roof over their heads, they often ask:
O, city!
Are you ever wrenched by the very roots
In the name of so-called progress?"

Roots often are an integral part of a tree. Roots once destroyed will result in the cessation of the whole tree. The roots can also be considered as the centre which holds the tree. Once the centre is lost, things will fall apart. Jacinta in her words exclaims how the villages of Jharkhand are losing their prosperity as the youth is disappearing in the name of opportunity. Will they survive after cutting their roots? Will they actually be successful without the shadow of their roots? It is a palpable sense of loss and it will result in the demolition of the being.

"A Madua Sprout On The Grave
On a little mound of mud in the village
Has emerged a tiny madua sprout.
Not a mere mound it is, but a grave,
In which lies the dead remains
Of Sugna, perished of hunger and starvation.
Having soaked in the life-giving dew
That madua seed cringing in fear hitherto
Has now emerged from hiding.
His children squirm about
Watching seedlings of paddy sprout
On the long unlit earthen stove
In the cow dung smeared courtyard.
And his widow, famished and distraught,
Stares at the blackened bottom of the rice pot
Kept upturned, empty, unfed,
As if by fire of hunger charred.
Sugna's wife and children
Will this time not starve to death.
They will take their own lives instead.
For dying of hunger, they know too well,

> Stirs up no storms, does not sell.
> A suicide, on the other hand,
> Guarantees their corpse will make headlines,
> And probes into the whys and wherefores
> Will lead them to many more doors
> With stoves unlit and ovens gone cold."

Madua or ragi is the staple diet of Jharkhand. Madua was considered the food of the poor and sometimes considered the symbol of poverty. Tribal people used to celebrate the flourishing grain and madua was one of the important grains. It is the best-yielding crop and it is sometimes bitter in taste too. Though madua or ragi crops signify that the ground is full of nutrition. The madua grows only on rich land. Madua sprouting on the grave signifies that the dead body is now providing the richness to the ground to support the growth of this crop. The title itself shows the grimness of the condition. The farmers of these areas are still struggling to grow crops. Some are due to their poverty, and some are suffering as their lands are seized by the bigger corporations in the name of industrial development etc. The farmers are hungry and find it difficult to live in the dog-eat-dog world. The irony in this poem is that the reason why the family of Sugna died was starvation. After their death finally, they are giving rise to madua grain.

It is believed that the human body is made up of five elements of nature. Earth, water, fire, air and space are the five elements. The dew which is watering the madua sprout is also the result of the culmination of some of these elements. The connection is itself visible in how the body and nature are so related and yet so different.

The madua in this poem depicts the struggles of these communities of Jharkhand. The poverty, the starvation, the backwardness etc. This leads to the suicide of the farmers which is a common trend in this state. Are we so weak that we cannot support the voices of these people? The madua is also the hope for future generations that will find help and support. They will be able to destroy the hypocrisy of society. They will be able to abandon the malignant practices of inequality in society. The graves are always celebrated by decorating them with beautiful flowers but this grave has a madua sprouting. The madua is not beautiful, but it is important to fill the empty stomachs of the people. Nature is beautiful and also essential for our sustenance.

"**The Six-Lane Freeway Of Deceit**
Emerging from the forests of Saranda,

Gathering are people in a certain village.
Women with infants in slings on their backs,
The aged scaling the valley leaning on their staffs,
The young leaping over the hills,
And children counting the sakua trees as they walk.
They gather not for a protest march,
But a football tournament to watch,
Where a goat is to be the winner's trophy.
No sooner is a child
From her mother's milk weaned,
Than he is made a member
Of some youth club in Saranda,
While something else goes on behind the scenes.
A football instead of books is places in every hand
That may someday join in protestors
Against the illicit mining of their land.
To win goats as tournament trophies
Kicked to the curb are books and studies.
Slowly but steadily the child inhales
The addicting opium of football.
Eyes, dazed and deadened by the game,
Fail to see beyond victory and loss
Their strife and struggle for survival.
Agents of mining corporations
Knock on every village door.
And no sooner is uttered a desperate sigh of hunger,
Than disease, unemployment and helplessness,
Are shoved down their throats
Grains, medicines, utensils, and clothes.
And the family carried away
As labourers, for a pittance pay.
In the name of progress, now
There are to be four and six-lane roads.
But those labouring away on concrete and asphalt
Are unaware. They know not
How many more free lanes of deceit
Run through the forests of Saranda."

The forest of Saranda is a disputable land in Jharkhand. Saranda forest or sal forest is a beautiful forest spread around Jharkhand which is beautiful and maintains the ecological balance in Jharkhand. This forest is also found to be the highest producer of coal. To protect these forests, the Maoists have spread around them and ensure that it is safe from the hands of the big commercial corporations or the government. It is also considered as the home for various wildlife animals who live freely here without any bondages. Saranda means elephant and it gets this name after the large number of elephants living in this forest. It is also considered the home of unique flying lizards.

As years passed, this Sal forest has now gained recognition as the symbol of freedom, prosperity and the fight for justice for the people of these communities. They have constantly tried to protect their forest and consider it an integral part of their identity. This forest signifies their comfort and safe place. They worship the forest. The poet mentioning the ongoing conflict through this symbol shows the oppression, the struggle and the brawl these communities are having. They might be strongly defending themselves but still, there are people who have been lured into the poisonous attempts by big-scale commercial corporations. The hunger is growing, the helplessness is growing and unemployment has always been the trouble faced by these people. They are still standing in this forest land and supporting the land, but are continuously forced to give up. They want to take shelter in their abode. These trees signify the freshness of their birthplace. These trees are the calm shadow of the ancestors. These forests are their home and their life. The generations are bestowed to protect this forest land and they will continue to do that further.

<u>**"THE RIVER, THE MOUNTAIN AND THE BAZAAR**</u>
We're here at the bazaar!
What would you like to buy, the shopkeeper asked.
Brother, a little rain, a handful wet earth,
A bottle of river, and that mountain preserved
There, hanging on the wall, a piece of nature as well.
And why is the rain so dear, pray tell?
The shopkeeper said - Their wetness is not of here!
It comes from another sphere.
Times are slack, have ordered just a sack."

The title of this poem itself shows the contrast between two realities. The rain and the mountain are natural creations while the bazaar or shops is a manmade creation. The customer goes to the bazaar (manmade creation) to ask for rain and a mountain (which is a natural creation). This piece shows how humans have continuously destroyed natural habitats for materialistic creations and industrial gains. The absurdity is that they consciously are aware of the after-effects of the ludicrous decision and they still are continuing with this. The parley is whether we should wait for the other generations to fight for their breath and live comfortably now or we should ourselves join hands for a better future.

These words 'A little rain' in the poem considers rain as the symbol of rebirth, prosperity, breaking of drought etc. The rain helps the lush green forest to smile. The rain refills the river and the earth gets refreshed after being wet. Rain is paramount for the life to sustain. The rain has always been the hero in many literary works. In the Mahabharat, the rain saves the people from dying of hunger. Just a little rain will be enough for the boy to return to his prosperous and happy life. River symbolizing life, freedom and fertility again is an important part of tribal communities. They have Koel, Swarnrekha (the river of gold), Mayurakshi river etc. which are losing their essence because of less rainfall received. The less rainfall is because of the abundant deforestation due to coal mining and industrialisation. The river is drying and so the mountains look lonely now without the river flowing from them. They want the river to be preserved. The mountain which is a symbol of strength should now be refreshed again. The rain which is responsible for beautiful rivers and rivers which end up making the mountains mesmerising completes the picture which these tribal communities live for. The complete cycle is impending in their dreams. They wish to achieve this dream as soon as possible. The times are slack but they are yet not satisfied with just a sack.

"Closed Doors

.... At dawn when the sun

Comes knocking at the door,

The darkness suffocating inside

To escape through the holes writhes,

And through those chasms she sees

A piece of the open sky

And the rays of the sun spread out to dry

In the courtyard

Like a bundle of paddy golden ripe......"

This particular poem shows the injustice faced by the woman of these tribal communities. The doors are closed for them and they are unable to open these doors of strong patriarchal practices in the tribal communities. The sun rising signifies hope for the women. The darkness behind the door is now dispersed a little. That sunlight comes as a hope to her to do away with the darkness hidden inside her and which is shadowing her. The open sky signifies the freedom she thirsts for. It is very lavish for her but she wants her sky too now. She wants to free herself from the bondage of society.

Kerketta has always talked about how she has witnessed her mother walking behind her father at social events. She used to eat after feeding her husband and the family. No matter how delayed her dinner gets, she used to wait. Kerketta has always resisted and condemned these practices in her works and speeches. This poem is the picture drawn by her to show the oppression faced by women and the darkness in the life of these tribal women.

Let her find the sky and the ray of sun she is looking for. Let her diminish the darkness and free herself from bondage.

Tribals of Jharkhand have faced a lot. They are still suffering from letting their voices be heard. They are still waiting for the miracles to happen. The aboriginals of Jharkhand have consistently protested to make this state beautiful. Their active participation can never be disregarded in history and contemporary times. The Munda, Oraon etc. are the reasons why Jharkhand is still considered a rich place of flora and fauna. They worship and understand the necessity of nature.

Jacinta Kerketta in her book not only raised the voices but touched on issues which are continuously faced by the people of Jharkhand. The suicide of the farmer, the class divide, the inequality, the patriarchy etc. which is still engraved in the ways of these communities. She wants to raise awareness and strongly condemn the evil of society. She works towards uplifting the lifestyle of these people and making them more aware of their rights. In her poems, she keeps on highlighting the evils of society. She has beautifully drawn parallels between the dreams of the people and nature. She has successfully portrayed the struggles of the people through her poems while keeping nature as the centre.

Nature has always been accepted as pure, serene, and calm on the one hand and wild, savage, and raging on the other hand. Nature as a symbol is evidently being used in the literature. Though Kerketta used this symbol to present the ignored and flouted communities of Jharkhand. She has outrageously spoken about these people,whether it be their freedom which was signified by the imagery of the sky or their struggles portrayed by the forest. The image of the river was been used to depict the fluidity required for the sustenance of life. She has carefully planted these symbols to let the readers contemplate the importance of nature and hear the voices too. The poems have one unifying voice though- it caters to the different issues faced by the people. Living in a world that institutionalises our every move, we should move towards the institution of nature and its conservations. Also, we should hear the outspoken and support them.

References

Kerketta, Jacinta. *Angor.* Adivaani Publications. 2016. Jharkhand. Print.

Kerketta, Jacinta. "Complete works of Jacinta Kerketta." Hindawi.https://www.hindwi.org/poets/jacinta-kerketta/all. Web.

Yadav, Anumesha. "The anger of Adivasis turns to poetry of anguish and hope in a young woman's hands." Scroll.in, June 05, 2016. https://scroll.in/article/808591/the-anger-of-adivasis-turns-to-poetry-of-anguish-and-hope-in-a-young-womans-hands. Web.

About The Editors

DR. SUDIP BHUI

    Sudip Bhui, M.Sc (Social-Cultural Anthropology), M.Sc. (Botany), M.Phil (Social Anthropology), Ph.D. (Medical Anthropology), (b. 1977)is presently working as Assistant Professor (Stage-III), Department of Anthropology and Tribal Studies. His research interest covers a vast area of tribal ethnography, identity and migration, indigenous knowledge, ethno-medicine, performing arts, Chhau dance, folk media, and communication; especially he is doing his fieldwork and innovative social services in Eastern India. He composed three books as Co-author, edited ten books and published more than sixty research articles. He has completed seven research Projects (one on Chhau Dance) and one is ongoing. Communication, mobilization and motivation of minority sections capable him to skilled agent in understanding, preserve and dignified Tribal culture.

DR. SAVITA MISHRA

Dr. Savita Mishra is a Principal, Vidyasagar College of Education, Phansidewa, Darjeeling, West Bengal. She has impeccable records of nineteen years of teaching and research activities. She has written more than hundred fifty research articles in reputed National and International journals and authored 67 books. She has also developed a psychological tool for assessing Attitude towards Science. She is the National resource person & Master trainer of MGNCRE, Ministry of Education, Government of India. She has awarded Best Teacher Award 2010 from Sikkim central University, Best Principal award 2020, Best Academician Award 2020, Celebrity writer award 2020, Excellent Achiever award 2020, Women Researcher Award 2021, Best Teacher Award (Higher Education) 2021, India Prime Top 100 Women Icon Award 2021 and Outstanding Scientist Award 2021. She has been conferred the title of 'Leading Educationists of the World' by IBC, Cambridge, London.

DR. SANJAY KUMAR CHOUDHARY

Dr. Sanjay Kumar Choudhary (b. 1969) obtained double MA (Political Science and Gandhian Thought), Ph.D.; currently he is National Coordinator, Chhau Kendra, Chandankiyari, Jharkhand, Sangeet Natak Akademi (SNA); Member, General Council, SNA, New Delhi, and was Ex-Member of Executive Body, ICH(UNESCO), Under Ministry of Culture, Government of India. Popularity as excellent anchor, socio-cultural activist, a believer of Gandhian Philosophy is brought him as icon. As thinker and policy maker he has intensive involvement with tribal language, culture and their morality development especially in rural area of Eastern India. He in his mission as cultural administration keeps a strong network for Chhau and Paika dance of Eastern India fetch him a series of awards and acknowledgements. He worked hard with SNA for poor, destitute, affected artists during COVID-19 period. Credit of a good number of research articles in popular research journals, edited volume and periodicals are glittered in his crown.

About The Book

We are celebrating the 'Amrit Kal' with all sections, communities of India. Tribal people of India are remaining heuristic subject for scholars, planners, developer and administrators. Editors and contributors made their utmost efforts to provide new dimensions for think about our tribal brethren. Our autochthonous people are responsible for building the resources, culture, and morality of ancient India. Now we can found tribal nation builders serve our India by their glory of indigenous knowledge in agriculture, medicine, environment, literatures and all around our practical life. Research and innovations for future India are essentially depends upon tribal scholars in the sectors of science, technology, space, sports, polity and clinical domain also. This volume will definitely help to bring new ideology, thoughts and actions for future researchers.

List Of The Contributors

Anima Besra: Student, Department of Anthropology and Tribal Studies, S K B University, Purulia, West Bengal, mabesra653@gmail.com; 8509568489

Nayan Ruhidas: Research Scholar of Anthropology & Tribal Studies, Sidho Kanho Birsha University, Purulia

nayanruhidas99@gmail.com; 8617387520

Piu Mahali: Research Scholar of Anthropology & Tribal Studies, Sidho Kanho Birsha University, Purulia

piumahali13@gmail.com; 7001821072

Pragya Jha: Doctoral Research Scholar, Presidency College, Chennai, pragya.stu@gmail.com;9953302409

Rajnarayan Podder: Doctoral Research Scholar, Department of Anthropology and Tribal Studies, S K B University, Purulia, West Bengal,rajnarayanpodder92@gmail.com; 9563831639

Samir Chandra Kuiri: Department of Chhau, Sidho Kanho Birsha University, Purulia, West Bengalsamirkuiry69@gmail.com; 6294329841

Sanjay Kumar Choudhary: Cultural Administrator and Social activist, sanjay.sankrit2000@gmail.com; **8210882356**

Savita Mishra: Principal, Vidyasagar College of Education Phansidewa, Darjeeling, West Bengal, India

mishrasavita.hce@gmail.com;9434409857

Sudip Bhui: Assistant Professor (Stage-III), Department of Anthropology and Tribal Studies,S K B University, Purulia, West Bengal. bhuisudip@gmail.com: 8016140737

Tarak Mohan Hazari: Doctoral Research Scholar, Department of Anthropology and Tribal Studies, S K B University, Purulia, West Bengal, tarakmohanhazari@gmail.com; 8250000279

Usharani Mahato: Doctoral Research Scholar, Department of Anthropology and Tribal Studies, S K B University, Purulia, West Bengal, usharanimahato29@gmail.com; 8617065487

9 7 9 8 8 8 8 6 9 1 8 1 6